# A HANDBOOK FOR GARDEN DESIGNERS

Rosemary Alexander FRSA
with Karena Batstone

CASSELL
ILLUSTRATED

First published in the UK in 1994 by Ward Lock
A Cassell imprint

Reprinted 1994
First paperback edition 1996
Reprinted 1998, 1999, 2000

This edition published in 2005 by Cassell Illustrated
a division of Octopus Publishing Ltd
2-4 Heron Quays
London E14 4JP

Distributed in the United States
by Sterling Publishing Co. Inc.
387 Park Avenue South, New York, NY 10016-8810

A British Library Cataloguing in Publication Data
block for this book may be obtained from the
British Library

ISBN 1 84403 370 8
EAN 9781844033706


Printed in China

Moreton Morrell Site

I's c

# A HANDBOOK FOR
# GARDEN DESIGNERS

# Contents

**Acknowledgments**
The authors would like to thank all who have helped in compiling this book, in particular the staff, tutors and students at the English Gardening School, especially Diana Abbott for typing and retyping the text. We also thank those who have allowed us to design their gardens – the plans for many of which appear here, and the following, whose work has been used in this book:

Alan Bartlett (p.123); Peter Beardsley (p.20); Georgina Bryson (pp.63, 79, 103); Elizabeth Cochrane (p. 101); Hallie Cohn (p. 96); Anthony du Gard Pasley (p.104); Lesley Faux (p.130); Ayuko Inoue (p. 119); IPC Magazines Ltd/Robert Harding Syndication/National Trust (p. 104); Sarah Janson (p. 63); Fred Jennett (pp. 17, 18); Pamela Lane-Smith (pp. 77, 82, 102); Gwyn Lewis (p. 108); Candace Long Brewer (pp. 99, 109); Helen Miller (pp. 80, 97); Rachel Myers (pp.73, 129); Tara Owens (p. 78); Ann Springford (p. 63); Susanna Yeatman Biggs (p. 119).

# Preface

In writing this book, we have tried to explain the surveying, draughting and planning techniques that we use as garden designers, and that we teach at the English Gardening School in London. No two designers will work in exactly the same way, and the intention of this book is to show what should be done, and how to do it, although we anticipate that most readers will adapt our suggestions to their own needs and environment.

In the past, garden plans were drawn individually for each client or garden, the work being executed in ink by skilled draughtsmen on cartridge paper as copying machines were not available. Today original work can be easily reproduced and all work, including the design process, must be carried out quickly and efficiently, as time spent on a project by the designer will be reflected in the client's bill.

We have tried to show that, as in most professions, there are certain aids, such as the grid, which can help inspire the most inhibited designer. We have tried to show simple and speedy drawing techniques, and as we expect most of our readers to draw their own plans, we do not attempt to compete with the graphics of design consultants who may employ specialists to execute their beautiful and often complex plans.

After understanding and experimenting with your own drawings, we hope you will become more critical and analytical of the work of other designers, often adapting a particular technique to your own style. We hope you enjoy your work, and that we may help you to express your intentions clearly to persuade your clients to build beautiful gardens.

Rosemary Alexander

Karena Batstone

# Introduction

Garden design is not simply a matter of choosing plants and arranging them on site. It is the culmination of a process that begins with the soil and the seasons and that involves everything from the construction of the garden to the way in which the client will use the space.

Although garden design is now a recognized profession, many of the most admired gardens, such as Sissinghurst in England, were laid out not by garden designers but by the owners of the properties themselves. Other gardens have evolved gradually, consecutive owners making alterations according to their needs or tastes. Frequently, fashion plays a part in these changes, people being influenced by magazines, television and other media. The increasing number of people visiting gardens over recent years has led to a greater interest in gardening and in garden design, with people trying to create in their own gardens what they have admired elsewhere. In Britain, many private gardens are open to the public, allowing other people to see what has been done and to ask how and why.

Home owners are now aware that a garden that is well laid out and well planted is an asset to be enjoyed and exploited, rather than a luxury to be considered if time and resources allow. These home owners may have admired the gardens of their friends and neighbours, but they are often themselves inexperienced in horticulture or too busy to design and plant their own gardens.

Garden centres can offer the materials, tools and plants, but the staff, even if they are qualified to do so, can rarely spare the time to visit the site and advise on garden layout. Home owners who want to redesign their gardens would save both time and money by calling in a garden designer, who will plan the space according to a client's requirements and the limitations of the site. Garden designers are often also used by house or hotel developers and by interior designers, who realize that their specialist expertise can greatly enhance a property.

Normally a garden designer will be responsible not only for designing the garden but also for suggesting a competent firm of builders to construct it. The designer will usually oversee the work, liaising with the owner about any alterations to the plan, supervising the planting and arranging for future maintenance. In some cases the clients may want only a planting plan or they may wish to construct the garden themselves, and most designers are accustomed to complying with the individual requirements of their clients. In many cases a designer will continue to advise a client as the garden develops.

# CHAPTER ONE

# Necessary equipment

In order to communicate ideas to a client the designer will usually survey the site and then draw up the survey to scale as the basis for a future design. Both surveying and draughting equipment will be necessary, and although a professional surveyor may sometimes be used, the designer will learn much more about the site by executing the survey.

## SURVEYING EQUIPMENT

You will need:

- **30m (100ft) tape measure,** preferably the modern, plasticized version, or two measures if the site is large (1)
- **metal skewer** secured with wire to the end of the tape
- **damp cloth** for cleaning the tape
- **2m (6ft) or 10m (33ft) rigid spring tape or measuring rod** for taking short dimensions, such as the height of steps or low walls (2)
- **double clip board** to keep out the wind or rain when making notes
- **graph paper** to help keep the lines straight when taking measurements (3)
- **note book**, A4 (11$\frac{2}{3}$ x 8$\frac{1}{4}$in) (4)
- **pencils, eraser and pens** (5)
- **ball of smooth, thick string** for setting out lines that may be too long for the tape measure, plus garden canes (6)
- **spirit level, pegs and a wooden plank** if simple levelling is required (7)
- **digital or SLR camera**, spare film and batteries, and a tripod (optional) (8)
- **compass** to ascertain north (9)
- **existing plans**, maps and plans for any proposed house extension or conservatory if available (10)
- **trowel and plastic bags and labels** for taking soil for pH testing (11)
- **suitable clothing**, warm and waterproof if necessary
- **bag** or holdall to keep all the equipment clean and dry

*Right: Surveying equipment.*

## HOW TO USE THE EQUIPMENT

**Tape measure** Before you buy a tape measure, make sure that all measurements are clear and easy to read and that the tape itself is strong and winds in easily. At the end of the tape there is usually a metal ring or hook, which can be slipped over a cane, hooked on to something or held by an assistant. Make sure that you count this ring as part of the measurement, otherwise all your dimensions will be slightly out. Keep the tape clean by always winding it in between a piece of damp cloth so that any dirt or dust picked up from the site is removed. If this is not done the inside of the case can easily become clogged. If you are unfamiliar with using a tape measure, practise measuring simple heights and widths and noting them down. In this way you will become familiar with the figures and will be less likely to make mistakes when measuring a real site.

**Metal skewer** This should be about 150mm (6in) long and should be fastened with wire or string to the ring or hook at the end of the tape. It can then be stuck into any convenient crack or into the soil or lawn and obviates the need for an assistant to hold the end of the tape measure.

**Rigid spring tape** This is particularly useful and quick for measuring vertical dimensions, such as steps or walls, where a long tape measure would be inconvenient. Again, take care to avoid getting dirt inside the casing.

**Double clip board** This is invaluable for protecting notes, graph paper or plans from

wind or rain when you are on site, because the upper side can be used as a shield when you are writing notes. A tough, plasticized, wipe-clean material is preferable.

**Graph paper** Buy paper that has reasonably large and clear squares and subdivisions rather than feint-ruled paper, which is difficult to read. If the site is small it is quite possible to draw it to scale while you are surveying by marking each major square as 1, or even 5 metres (yards) and using the subdivisions to write down the actual measurements. An A4 ($11\frac{2}{3}$ x $8\frac{1}{4}$in) or A3 ($16\frac{1}{2}$ x $11\frac{2}{3}$in) pad is recommended.

**Notebook** Ideally, this should have lined paper and be fairly sturdy.

**Pencils, eraser and pens in plastic case** An assortment of these, in good working order, is useful because different colours can be used to denote different things, making the survey notes easier to read and transcribe.

**Ball of smooth string** In larger gardens some dimensions may be too long to take with a tape measure. If you set up a dimension line with string and garden canes you can take the measurements by running the tape measure along the string and marking each 30 metres (yards) or so off on it. You will find this is particularly useful when you are triangulating across a large site.

**Spirit level, pegs and wooden plank** These are useful for gauging minor changes in level, such as a gentle slope across a garden. By setting up the pegs, balancing the plank on them and then checking with a spirit level, slight changes can be assessed without using expensive surveying equipment. Surveying equipment, such as a dumpy level or a theodolite, can be hired if necessary.

**Camera, spare film and batteries** Almost any digital or SLR camera will suffice, but an adjustable, wide angle/standard lens is very useful. Film must be suited to the climatic conditions, to what is being photographed and to the purpose for which the photographs are to be used. A tripod is useful for producing more professional photographs.

**Existing plans** If they are available these can save hours of measuring and drawing. Architects' plans can be reduced or enlarged as necessary and are very accurate. Maps drawn to scales of 1 : 1250 or 1 : 12500 are too small to be accurate when enlarged, although they can be used as the basis for a more accurate survey.

**Compass** You will need to be able to ascertain the north, which will, in turn, determine sunny and shady areas within the garden.

**Trowel, plastic bags and labels** You will need to take soil samples to be tested for their pH levels. Each sample should be clearly labelled, to indicate from exactly where it was taken.

**Warm and waterproof clothing** Although this may seen obvious, waterproof clothing is often overlooked. Surveying can be a cold, lengthy operation, and it will seem more so if you are unsuitably dressed.

## DRAWING EQUIPMENT

You will need:
- **drawing board**, A1 ($33\frac{1}{8}$ x $23\frac{1}{2}$in) or A2 ($23\frac{1}{2}$ x $16\frac{1}{2}$in) size, with parallel motion
- **tracing paper**, A1 ($33\frac{1}{8}$ x $23\frac{1}{2}$in) or A2 ($23\frac{1}{2}$ x $16\frac{1}{2}$in) size and smaller
- **graph paper**, ($33\frac{1}{8}$ x $23\frac{1}{2}$in) or A2 ($23\frac{1}{2}$ x $16\frac{1}{2}$in) size and smaller
- **technical drawing pens** of nib sizes 0.7, 0.5, 0.35 and 0.25 plus black specialist ink (1)
- **felt-tip pens or drawing markers** (2)
- **graphite pencils** with HB and B leads, or clutch pencil and leads, or 0.5mm constant-width pencils (3)
- **pencil sharpener**
- **eraser** for ink and pencil (4)
- **erasing shield** for precision erasing (5)
- **scalpel and razor blades** for scratching out (6)
- **set-squares** – 90º/45º and 30º/60º (7)
- **masking tape** (8)
- **adjustable set-square** with angle scale
- **compasses** with extension arm and ink attachment (9)
- **metric scale** to include 1 : 1, 1 : 50, 1 : 100, 1 : 200, 1 : 1250, 1 : 2500
- **circle template** with bevelled edges for ink work (10)
- **drawing board brush or duster** (11)
- **flexi-curve**, at least 300mm (12in) long (12)
- **plastic tube** for carrying drawings

For lettering and colouring up:
- **lettering stencils** to fit pen sizes (optional) (13)

*Right: Draughting equipment.*

- **coloured pencils** or watercolours for colouring up plans (14)
- **rolling ruler** to guide handwriting (15)

## HOW TO USE THE EQUIPMENT

**Drawing board** Drawing boards are made to correspond with the standard drawing paper sizes. The board can be as basic or as sophisticated as you like. Use a laminated board with parallel motion (a sliding horizontal ruler), which can be either table mounted or free standing. All types of drawing board should have faces that are perfectly flat and smooth, so that they will not twist or buckle with normal use. Edges should be at right-angles to one another. Do not stick drawing pins into your board or use it for cutting because you may harm the surface. For ink work, it is easier to draw accurately on an angled surface. You may need to try several different positions before you find the most comfortable angle.

**Tracing paper** It is useful to have several sizes, although if you buy A1 (33⅛ x 23½in) sheets you can always cut them down. They can be bought in pads or in single sheets and in various weights – for example, 60gsm, 90gsm and 120gsm – or in rolls. You will throw a lot of tracing paper away while you are working up a design, and so it is advisable to use the lightest, 60gsm, until your design is finalized – the lighter the weight, the cheaper the paper. You can then do your final drawing on a slightly heavier weight. Until you know the size you are most likely to use – you are unlikely to use A1 (33⅛ x 23½in) unless you are doing a design for a large garden – buy the paper in sheets of A2 (23½ x 16½in). You can always buy an A4 (11⅔ x 8¼in) pad for small sketches.

**Paper** You can buy this as you go along but in the first instance you will need one or two sheets of A1 (33⅛ x 23½in) metric graph paper. You will not draw on this, but it will be the first sheet of paper to be put on your board and will serve as your backing sheet.

**Technical drawing pens** These are required for drawing with ink on tracing paper, but do not use them on ordinary paper because the nibs will become clogged. The pens are expensive to buy, and you will have to practise to get even lines. The nibs come in a variety of sizes, which correspond to the thickness of line – 0.25, 0.35, 0.5 and 0.7 are the most useful – and extra nibs can be bought. The pens must be properly looked after so that they do not become clogged with ink. They should be held upright against the parallel motion or set-square so that the ink flows evenly. Use a smooth, even pressure to draw all lines. An alternative to technical pens are the disposable drawing pens that are now available.

**Set-square** This triangle of, usually, clear plastic is used for vertical and diagonal line drawing when rested on the edge of the parallel motion. Get the largest size you can or will have trouble drawing long vertical lines. The length of the longest side should be around 250–300mm (10–12in). If you intend to do your final drawing in ink, make sure you buy a set-square that has angled edges, which help to eliminate smudging. You will need both a 45° angle set-square and an adjustable set-square and an adjustable set-square to carry out axonometric drawing. For isometric drawing a 30°/60° set square is necessary.

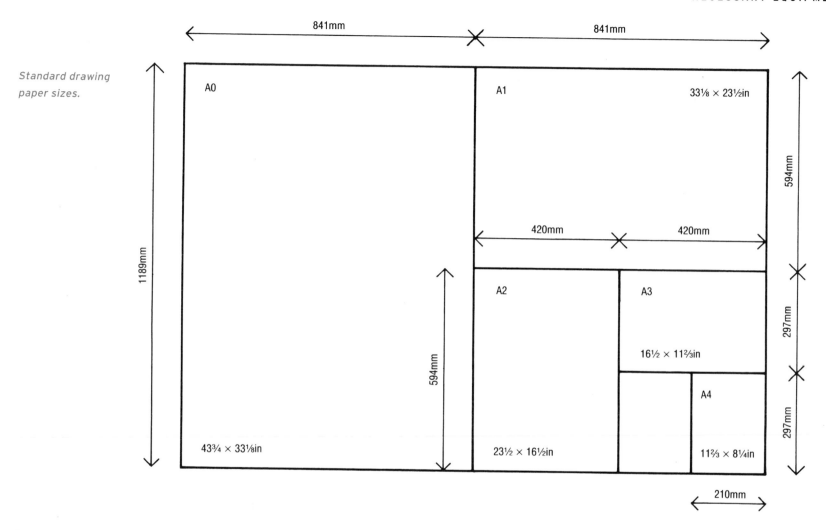

*Standard drawing paper sizes.*

**Compasses** You will need a pair of compasses for drawing up your survey and for larger circles and curves. Purchase a pair with an extension arm for doing the survey and for making large circles, plus an ink attachment for working up final drawings.

**Pencils and pens** It is useful to have a selection of pencils with graphite leads varying in degrees of hardness and softness, although you will usually need HB and B. The cost of the pencil will be proportionate to its usefulness. Cheap pencils have gritty, crumbly leads, which smudge. Hard lead tends to eat into the surface of the paper. The most useful grades are H (hard), used for technical drawing, HB and 2B (soft), used for freehand drawing and 3B, which is used for shading. An alternative to the ordinary pencil is the fine-lead pencil, a form of 'clutch' pencil, which does not require sharpening as the diameter of the lead represents the point size. A 0.5mm diameter is the easiest to use. Other types of clutch pencil are also available, but these require an appropriate sharpener to keep the point sharp.

**Coloured pencils/water soluble pencils**
There are some excellent brands, but the colours need to be carefully chosen so that they are appropriate for garden design – use natural shades and pastels, rather than bright or harsh colours.

**Scales** Scales are narrow strips of plastic the length of a normal ruler and either flat or triangular in shape. They have varying numbers of divisions along each edge on both sides. The divisions are in proportion to actual distances and dimensions and are used for making plans drawn to scale. The scales most often used are 1 : 50 and 1 : 100, but most scales go up to at least 1 : 1250 or 1 : 2500. If you wish to work in imperial scale the nearest equivalent to 1 : 50 and 1 : 100 is ¼in : 12in and ⅛in : 12in. The use of a scale rule is much easier in practice than it is in theory.

**Pencil sharpeners** To draw accurately it is most important that you sharpen pencil leads frequently. Any type of pencil sharpener can be used, but often an ordinary pen knife and sandpaper produces the best results. The point can be rounded with the sandpaper so that it does not cut into the paper and so that it wears away evenly and remains a constant distance from any straight edge.

**Eraser** This should be a combination of soft rubber for erasing pencil work and a special composition rubber, which removes ink without damaging the surface of the paper. The accumulated small particles of rubber should be brushed or dusted off the paper.

**Erasing shield** This thin piece of metal is laid over the drawing to mask anything that is not intended for erasure.

**Drawing board brush or duster** You will need a simple soft brush or duster to keep drawings clean by removing graphite dust or eraser shavings from them. Sweep your drawings regularly as you work on them.

**Circle template** This useful device has 20 or 30 different sized circles for drawing small circles, such as pots of avenues of trees. Make sure that the largest circle is about 5mm (2in) in diameter. A bevelled edge is useful to prevent ink smudges, and if several circles of the same size are to be drawn, it is helpful to mark this circle with a small piece of masking tape so that the wrong size is not used in error.

**Flexi-curve** A hollow strip of plastic filled with a bendable metal strip is useful as a guide for drawing curves. The pen or pencil must be carefully rested upon the flexible shape and smooth, even pressure applied.

**Plastic tube** When you transport drawings to the printers or to clients you will need to protect them

**Scalpel and razor blades** Although you will use your eraser to remove most mistakes or revisions, a scalpel and blades will probably also be necessary. The blade should be curved, not pointed, as it is much easier to use and will do less harm to the surface of the paper. Remember to rub the damaged paper surface with an eraser to restore it, otherwise the

technical pen ink will 'bleed' or the lines will appear too thick.

## For lettering or colouring

**Stencils** Lettering templates or stencils will act as a guide for pens. A variety of sloping and upright styles are available, and, although practice is needed in using them, stencils are very useful if you want to make certain headings stand out. They are also useful when several people work on a drawing but the handwriting must remain uniform.

**Non-photo pencil** Use these pencils to draw guidelines on plans. These lines will not print and will not, therefore, need to be erased.

**Coloured pencils and watercolours** There are so many of these to choose from that it is wise to experiment until you find a medium that suits your style and capability. Whether you use simple children's crayons in basic colours or pastels or watercolour, the application of colour to a drawing can enliven the effect and make the drawing easier to understand.

**Rolling ruler** A 300mm (12in) strip of transparent plastic attached to a roller, useful as a guide for neat free-hand notes.

## LETTERING AND TITLING ON DRAWINGS

Almost every drawing will require the addition of some descriptive words or notes to clarify the meaning, but if the lettering lacks confidence, it can seriously undermine what may otherwise be an effective drawing. It is worthwhile developing a particular style, which will then be used on all your work.

The garden designer ought to be proficient in three different types of lettering, as a combination of the three will be used on most plans and title blocks. These are freehand lettering, stencil or guided-pen lettering and computer-generated lettering.

For speed and consistency most notes on a drawing should be written freehand, in either pencil or pen depending on the medium that has been used for the drawing, or use computer-generated labelling. Stencils or guided-pen lettering may be used for headings and titles. Whatever you decide to use, you should aim to achieve:

- consistency
- legibility
- style
- spacing
- speed

Strive for consistent letter forms, consistent spacing between letters and words, consistent style and a consistent line weight.

The legibility of your work will depend on the shape and form of each letter, the spacing between the letters, the way in which the words are arranged and the variation of the sizes and positions of lettering according to their importance. An overexaggerated style can be as difficult to read as an under-exaggerated one.

Copy and experiment and choose what is comfortable for you. Do not exaggerate or get too stylistic. Remember to keep the lettering legible and bear in mind that acceptable styles are vertical or slanted forwards, vertical being more commonly used.

Aim for close spacing between letters in a words and wider spacing between words. Spacing between lines of lettering will depend on how much space is available, but spacing can be fairly close, with more space left between paragraphs. The longer the line, the greater the spacing between those lines should be.

It is necessary to develop a style that can be executed quickly, while still remaining consistent and legible. Freehand writing is always quicker than using stencils.

Before you experiment with lettering, examine your own natural style. Is it upright or sloping? Try to adapt your natural style to the freehand writing that you will use on plans. The stencil can be in the same style, or it can be a complete contrast, which may relieve monotony on a drawing, making the notes easier to read. The size of the letters should be based on the importance of the notes on the drawing.

*This style of lettering is quick to draw and easy to read.*

ABCDEFGHIJKLMNOPQRSTUVWXZY
abcdefghijklmnopqrstuvwxyz
1234567890

TO AID LEGIBILITY AVOID
VARYING THE LETTER HEIGHT
VARYING THE LETTER SPACING
VARYING THE LETTER WEIGHT
VARYING THE LETTER SLANT

For presentation work, it is helpful to place a fresh sheet of tracing paper over the drawn plan, mapping out the notes around the different elements to strengthen the overall composition. It is better to organize the notes in blocks rather than to splatter them over the entire sheet. When you have decided exactly what you want to say and where it will be located, this tracing paper overlay can be placed under the plan, to act as a guide for the final lettering.

## Freehand lettering guidelines

To achieve clear, consistent lettering, always use guidelines. These are thin, horizontal lines drawn lightly, either in pencil on the final sheet, to be erased later, or on a sheet that is placed under the final drawing. If a non-photo pencil is used to draw the guidelines directly on to the final sheet, it will not reproduce when copied. The guidelines will help you to maintain consistent letter dimensions and spacings.

To draw the guidelines begin by drawing the upper and lower lines, and then add the third line halfway between them. All crossbars should connect along this third line.

On most plans, irrespective of whether the lettering is completed in freehand or by stencil, only three or four sizes of letter are required. The actual size of the letters ought to be in proportion to the size of the sheet and to the type of drawing. Normally these three or four sizes will be used on most plans, so it may be worth taking time to draw up rows of the

*Guidelines will help to keep your lettering even in size and shape. The spacing between each line of words must also be consistent.*

guidelines in a fine ink line so that they can remain as an office 'tool' and be used as a guide behind all drawings.

Another short cut to lettering guides is to collect sheets of lined paper of varying dimensions, which can be slipped behind the final sheet, secured with masking tape and used as a backing for lettering. Even the actual gridded graph paper backing sheet can be used as a guide, but the 'three-line' guideline usually produces the best result. Always practise for a while before beginning the actual presentation lettering.

**Lining up lettering** For consistency and clarity, all lettering should be lined up to a margin or margins. This will ensure that the first letter of each new line follows exactly beneath the first letter of the preceding line. A similar margin, or end point, should occur at the opposite side, the effect being similar to that achieved on a typewriter or word processor. Again, these margin lines can be drawn in with a non-photo pencil.

**Underlining** Underlining certain lettering may help it to stand out, and when you draw any line, the emphasis should always be on the end-points of each line, avoiding the tendency to decrease pressure at the end of the stroke.

FOR EASY READING ALWAYS USE INVISIBLE MARGINS TO ORGANISE YOUR TEXT INTO BLOCKS OF EQUAL WIDTH WITHOUT THEM THE EYE IS LED ALL OVER
  THE PLACE AND THE READER IS DISTRACTED
 FROM THE MESSAGE OF THE TEXT

*Invisible margins should be used to align the first letter of each line.*

**Pencil weight** Keep the weights of pencil lines consistent and use an HB lead because an H lead will tend to bite into the paper and a B lead will tend to smudge. A small sheet of tracing paper can be used under your hand to prevent smudging. Always begin at the top of a sheet and work down, keeping the pencil weight consistent and sharpening the lead when necessary. After sharpening, the pencil lead may need to be worked or slightly blunted before it will look consistent with the work just executed.

In general, the verticals of letters should be drawn with a thin line, while the horizontals can be drawn boldly with thicker lines. The technique of using a small set-square to draw all vertical lines can also be effective but needs to be practised before it can be done quickly.

**Stencilling or guided-pen lettering**
Stencils can be used for titling drawings or notes and, when they are used properly, they will produce a clear, uniform result. They can be made of metal but are more usually clear plastic, sometimes with a fine metal supporting strip at both top and bottom.

Stencils are available in a wide range of lettering styles and sizes, but make sure that the chosen size will accommodate your nib size. Stencils are made in sizes to correspond with the nib size of technical ink pens, and if the nib size is large, it will not fit into the letters; if it is smaller, the nib will move about and produce uneven lettering. The stencil plate must be held firmly down with one hand against your parallel motion or T-square, while the other hand is used to hold the pen. The parallel motion or T-square must be held firmly, and the stencil moved backwards and forwards against it until the line is completed. The pen must be held in an upright position so that the ink flows freely. Spacing between letters must be done by eye, with closer spacing between letters and wider spacing between words.

At first, stencils may appear difficult to use, but with practise they can be quick and effective, and are very useful in producing uniformity in lettering when several people are working on a drawing, although similar spacing must be followed. The stencils should be kept clean and washed occasionally to prevent ink clogging the letters.

## THE USE OF COMPUTERS AND THE INTERNET

Although a computer is by no means an essential piece of equipment at any stage of the garden design process, more and more designers are using computers to assist them in research, presentation and communicating their ideas with clients and contractors.

For research and accessing data, the internet is invaluable. At the planting plan stage, for instance, it can be much more efficient to search the detailed plant databases published online by horticultural institutes, than use specialist books. Books do date and are expensive to replace. These databases provide an encyclopaedia of the most commonly used plants in cultivation, with information on a large number of attributes, such as height, spread and form, favoured site aspect and soil type. Some even offer suggestions for plant combinations.

A plant database enables you to search quickly for plants to meet any number of given requirements – for instance you can ask it to give you a list of all the plants that will thrive in a sandy soil, flower in June and have fragrant flowers. For offline research there are also plant databases available on disc. These can usually be customised, allowing you to add more plants to the list and alter any existing plant attributes if you don't agree with the publisher!

Increasingly, plant nurseries are publishing updated availability lists on their websites, and will email digital photographs of specimen plants. These facilities can save time when compiling plant lists and cut down on time-consuming nursery visits.

Basic computers with simple word processing facilities are relatively inexpensive and have many uses for the garden designer. For plan presentation, word processors can provide a huge range of fonts, or typefaces, that you can use to generate printed labels and keys. These can then be printed out onto adhesive film, cut to size and applied to a hand drawn plan for a professional looking finish.

Many new computers now come bundled with image-editing software (Photoshop and Photopaint, for example), which can be useful for experimenting with ideas. To visualise proposed changes in a garden for instance, you could import a photograph of the site into the programme, and then use drag and drop functions to superimpose images of trees, pergolas etc (either your own images scanned in, or accessed from a landscape image library) to build up the photomontage.

Garden designers working with others in the design and construction sectors, such as surveyors and architects, will find that surveys, plans and elevations are often produced digitally, using a graphic software programme such as vector-CAD (computer aided design) or vector-GIS (geographical information system). Although not essential, it can be useful to be able to read these files, if not manipulate them. For those that would like to draft their own plans on screen and create 3D models from the information provided, there are now bolt-on additions to the vector-CAD and vector-GIS programmes, specifically tailored for landscape designers. In addition to the drafting and modelling facilities the software can also simulate changes through time, what is often referred to as 4D design.

*Digital plans can be produced and adapted quickly,*
*and are easy to understand.*

For general office management there are now dedicated programmes for the garden designer for producing plant schedules, bills of quantity, and costings. All of the variables can be tailored to your own requirements. There are also programs that include time logs for project monitoring purposes and address databases.

Many garden designers now have their own website, to attract clients or raise the profile of the business. Typically, the website will provide information on design approach as well as portfolio information, such as details of completed projects with images where possible. The website may be designed 'in house' or contracted out to a specialist firm. Whichever way you do it, it is important to think about the key words that you will want to use to describe your practice as this is how the search engines will gain access to your website.

*CAD and other drawing programmes can be used to experiment with planting plans.*

- **Tellima grandiflora purpureum**
- **Liriope muscari**
- **Molinia caerulea variegata**
- **Narcissus February Gold**
- **Anemone blanda**
- **Fritillaria meleagris**

# CHAPTER TWO

# Preliminary arrangements

The initial enquiry from a possible client may be made by telephone, by letter or even through casual conversation over dinner. Too often, however, the client who wishes to have a garden redesigned does not realize what is involved, assuming that it is merely a question of obtaining a few plants and popping them in! Most designers are either properly trained, or have years of experience behind them – often both. They will, therefore, expect to be paid for passing on their expertise, and will work for a set hourly rate in the same way as any other professional, be it doctor, dentist or design consultant.

## ENQUIRIES FROM POTENTIAL CLIENTS

The initial enquiry is usually made in one of three ways:
• by letter
• by telephone
• through casual conversation

Too often, however, the client who wishes to have their garden redesigned does not realize what is involved, assuming that it is merely a question of obtaining a few plants and popping them in! The most realistic enquiries usually come through word of mouth, a new client seeking you out because they admire a garden that you have designed for a friend or colleague.

New clients may not realize that garden design is now a recognized profession and that many designers have undergone both a rigorous training and may have years of experience behind them. They will therefore expect to be paid for passing on their expertise and will work for a set fee in the same way as any other professional, be it architect, dentist or design consultant.

## SCALE OF FEES

Establish at the earliest stage what services you as a garden designer can offer and what and when you will expect to be paid. So that no misunderstanding can occur, make sure this is put in writing either in the form of a letter or as a printed card, perhaps with your identifying logo. The simplest way of doing this is to write down in logical order all the services that you are able to provide – from surveying to finding a contractor to build the garden, or to supply plants and plant it up.

## INCIDENTAL EXPENSES

Travelling time, fares, petrol and incidental expenses such as camera film or copies of drawings also need to be charged to the client. All receipts should be kept as proof of costs incurred. As each new job comes in, make up a client file which is divided up to contain the following documents:

• Time sheet
• Client brief with details of name, address etc. plus what is wanted and by when
• Directions to site, maps, existing plans
• Correspondence with the client
• Correspondence with contractors or suppliers, such as estimates for work or plant orders
• Copies of your plans for the client's garden (NB the originals should be kept flat in a drawer or portfolio and should never be folded).

### Responding to an enquiry

So that your potential client understands what garden design can involve, your scale of fees should be sent well in advance of the first meeting, perhaps with a friendly covering note. Shortly before the meeting, a telephone call or email, ostensibly to confirm the time and date, can also be used to check whether the garden owner has received and is agreeable to the scale of fees. Be clear about the terms of this first consultation – some designers charge for their first visit, others do not, taking a gamble on later being offered the work; some clients will wish to meet several designers before deciding which might be most suitable to their needs.

### The first meeting

At the initial meeting it is critical that both client and designer will be able to establish a good working relationship – the garden owner respecting the knowledge and reputation of the designer and similarly, the designer's ability to interpret and fulfil the client's wishes or briefing. In some cases, the client may have chosen the designer because they admire the designer's work, or because they specialize in a particular style of garden. Take with you a portfolio of previous work to include 'before' and 'after' photographs. Showing the client your previous work, giving them a rough idea of how much the gardens cost to build, will broach the subject of budget or available funds and maintenance.

## VISITING THE SITE

Even if you are uncertain if you will be offered the job of redesigning the garden, it is sensible to be well prepared for this first meeting, even to the extent of adding an extra half-hour to the journey time to see other gardens in the neighbourhood. This will also give you an idea of what will or will not grow and will also therefore indicate soil type, climate and so on.

The site may be small and the clients may want you to survey the site on the first visit, so it is wise to travel with your surveying equipment and a portfolio of pictures of work

done for your previous clients. Clients often have an idea of what they do not want but are less clear about what they do want, and photographs and plans of other gardens make this easier to establish. Also, if you are fairly new to the profession, do not be afraid to admit it – your charges should reflect this and bluffing will only lead to later embarrassment!

When you arrive at the site, make notes on factors such as the locality – affluent or otherwise – the state of upkeep of the property – a clue to both the clients' personality and the available labour – the architectural style of the house and the age and period of the furnishings. The colour schemes, the pictures on the walls and even the kitchen will tell you a lot about the clients and their lifestyle. Look for any dominant features outside the house that you may wish to echo in the design of the garden.

Normally the client will walk around the garden with you, pointing out likes and dislikes, and things that are to be retained or discarded. You may not necessarily agree with all of this, but the preferences of the client are part of your brief, and time spent now finding out potential problems and preferences will save disagreement later. Often it is wise to have a second walk round the garden alone, your attention no longer being distracted, to assess the potential and also to think through the most mutually advantageous way of carrying out the work. While it is essential to convince the clients that you know exactly how to deal with the garden, do not go into too much detail at this stage lest they carry out your ideas themselves without employing you.

### Establishing a budget

A budget, or amount of money that the clients have available for the project, must also be established at an early stage. It may help to point out that a garden is like an outdoor room and that the budget allocated to it should be comparable to that set aside for an important room such as a kitchen. When it comes to establishing a budget your clients will want to know what they will get for their money. You should have a good idea of the costs of a range of materials as well as of likely laying and maintenance costs of those materials. Try also to have a figure for planting costs per square metre (yard) that includes the plants themselves and any soil conditioners, fertilizers and so forth that may be necessary plus the cost of labour required to prepare the ground and do the planting. Obviously this figure will vary according to your sources of plants and the kind of planting that the clients require – for example, the proportion of shrubs to herbaceous plants – as well as local labour charges.

Once these matters have been agreed, a follow-up letter stating your objectives can then be sent and if accepted, work can begin.

## CLIENT BRIEF

Client name(s): _____

Client address: _____

Site address (if different): _____

Telephone: Day: _____ Evening: _____ Mobile: _____

Fax: _____ Email: _____

Date of first contact: _____ Date of response: _____

Date of initial consultation meeting: _____

Date and time of briefing meeting: _____

### General

What do you want done?  Full design, hard landscaping, planting: _____

When was the house built (roughly): _____

### Client details

Number living at site address: _____

comprising: _____

Client's age(s): _____ Children _____ Age(s) _____

M/F_____

Pets: _____ Staff: _____

Does anyone who will use the garden have disabilities or allergies which will need to be considered during the design stage? Yes/No   Please describe: _____

_____

What time of day and on what days is the garden currently used most?_____

When and how do you use the garden at present, and are there regular periods when you are NOT there: _____

How do you want to use the space?_____

Entertaining/dining  Yes/No          If so for up to how many: _____

Barbecuing  Yes/No    Sitting (in sun)  Yes/No    (in shade)  Yes/No

Swimming/hot tub/jacuzzi  Yes/No    Working  Yes/No

Playing games (croquet etc.)  Yes/No    Children's play  Yes/No

Does playing require equipment, if so what equipment: _____

Do the children have any special (non-playing) activities which need to be

catered for? _____

### Practical considerations

Will any of the following be needed:

Compost heap  Yes/No    Shed/workshop/potting shed  Yes/No

Washing line  Yes/No

What sort of washing line: _____

Where is it at present? _____

Water butt  Yes/No    Outside tap  Yes/No    Garage  Yes/No

Access from garage through the site?  Yes/No

Access through site to street  Yes/No    Electrical supply  Yes/No  Explain

_____

Greenhouse  Yes/No    Conservatory  Yes/No

Parking space – if so for how many cars? _____

Is this set to change in the future  Yes/No

Dustbins  Yes/No    Do the bins need to be kept on site?

Where are they kept at present? _____

Is this convenient?  Yes/No  Explain: _____

Bonfire site  Yes/No    Special storage (if so for what): _____

Ramps/handrails  Yes/No

(if so for whom)_____

Anything else to be incorporated: _____

### Garden features

Which (if any) of these features would you like included in the garden?

Terrace (to accommodate how many and for what purpose)?_____

(in sun)  Yes/No    (in shade)  Yes/No

Lawn  Yes/No    Herb garden  Yes/No

Vegetable garden  Yes/No    Wildflower garden/meadow  Yes/No

Fruit trees  Yes/No    Soft fruit  Yes/No

Arches  Yes/No    Pergola  Yes/No    Gazebo  Yes/No

Summer house  Yes/No    Other buildings (studio, office, children's den)  Yes/No

Additional details: _____

Water feature(s)  Yes/No – if so what type: _____

Fountain  Yes/No    Formal pool  Yes/No    Informal pond  Yes/No

Rill  Yes/No    Stream  Yes/No    Waterfall  Yes/No

Additional details: _____

Lighting (if so what sort of lighting do you want incorporated?)

Security  Yes/No    Directional  Yes/No    Illuminating plants/trees  Yes/No

Ambient lighting Yes/No

Additional details: _____

Permanent barbecue  Yes/No    Mobile barbecue  Yes/No            Irrigation  Yes/No

**Materials to be used**

What materials are already used on site (on the house): _____

(in the garden): _____

Do you like these materials  Yes/No

What materials would you like used in the garden?

Gravel  Yes/No   Decking  Yes/No   Timber  Yes/No    Natural stone  Yes/No

Reconstituted stone  Yes/No   Recycled materials  Yes/No

Salvaged materials  Yes/No

Any other materials: _____

What materials would you not like used in the garden? _____

**Garden style**

Are there any garden styles you like?_____


How do you want the garden to look?  Neat/tidy  Yes/No

Full of plants  Yes/No   Cottage style  Yes/No   Traditional  Yes No   Formal  Yes/No

Informal  Yes/No   Contemporary  Yes/No   Minimalist  Yes/No

**Planting**

Spring colour  Yes/No    Summer colour  Yes/No    Autumn colour  Yes/No

Winter colour  Yes/No   All year colour  Yes/No   Scented  Yes/No

Attracts wildlife  Yes/No

Are there any plants you would or would not like included? _____

**Colour**

What colours do you like or not like? _____

Are there any colours (in the house) in rooms adjacent to the site, than can be used in

the garden?  Yes/No

If so what?_____

Interior décor (if relevant)    Modern  Yes/No   Traditional  Yes/No

Do you collect anything that you would like included in the garden?_____

**What can be retained on site?**

Are there any structural components within the garden that must be kept?  Yes/No

Are there any trees/plants that should be retained: _____

Boundaries, do you want to change any of the boundary fences/hedges/walls etc. (if so

client needs to check which are their boundaries/speak to neighbours etc). Yes/No

**Garden maintenance**

What level of expertise/interest do you have? _____

How many hours per week do you spend maintaining the garden at present? _____

How many hours per week do you **want** to spend maintaining the garden? _____

Are there any jobs you particularly enjoy doing in the garden? _____

Are there any jobs you dislike?_____

Do you have any physical infirmities that prevent you from doing certain jobs? _____

Is there anything that currently precludes your enjoyment of the garden (lack of

privacy, noise pollution?): _____

**Miscellaneous**

Are there any local authority constraints upon the site, TPO's, maximum wall/fence

heights, listed house, listed garden? _____

Are there any areas of the garden that are particularly:

Wet  Yes/No.  If so where? _____

Dry  Yes/No.  If so where? _____

Windy  Yes/No.  If so where?_____

Smelly  Yes/No.  If so  where?_____

Where is the most sheltered part of the garden?_____

Where is the least sheltered part of the garden?_____

Any other information you think is relevant: _____

_____

_____

_____

CHAPTER THREE

# The site survey

Before any serious work can begin on replanning a garden, an accurate survey of the site must be carried out so that a plan can be drawn up to show the existing solution. This plan should give the exact location of the various elements of the site indicating their height and width, and it should also show any changes in level. Although your clients may not wish to keep certain features, they should still be included in the survey, as any decision to retain, remove or re-site features will be made at a later stage.

## WHAT TO INCLUDE AND HOW TO PROCEED

The survey should include all measurable elements, not only the house and the boundaries of the garden, but also any features that may affect future planning – anything from drainpipes, manhole covers, electricity poles, changes in level, to existing trees and shrubs. It must also include notes on non-measurable elements, such as views out, orientation, prevailing winds, soil type and texture, all of which will influence the design and must be noted while on site.

The measured information will be used to draw up a scale plan of the site, and this plan will become the basis for all future work. It must therefore be accurate. If it is not, it could jeopardize any future plans by seriously distorting the eventual layout and probably inflating the cost of the garden unnecessarily. Clarity is essential when noting measurements, most mistakes being made by the measurer being unable to read or understand dimensions from his or her own notes.

A survey should include the following:

- the house, including doors and their direction of opening, and windows with sill heights
- existing man-made features – drains, vents, wall plants and any other elements along or close to the house wall; outbuildings, such as garages or sheds, should not be overlooked.
- boundaries formed by hedges, fences or walls, including the material as well as the height, width and position of any uprights, buttresses or gates, or other access points of openings
- major trees and shrubs, showing trunk, girth, height and spread, and plant names where possible
- low retaining walls, paths and steps, including their direction, height and width, and the material used
- any areas of water – pools, ponds, streams or lakes
- existing planting – flower beds, shrubs, trees or grass
- changes in level resulting from slopes or terraces
- drainage – the position of manhole covers and, if necessary, the septic tank
- the north point, or direction of the sun at noon in relation to the site
- features outside the property boundaries that may affect the garden – a neighbour's overhanging tree, for example
- non-measurable elements, such as views in and out, direction of prevailing winds, soil type and pH factor

It is, of course, possible to have a professional survey done by a land surveyor, but this is expensive and you will learn a great deal more about the site by doing the measuring yourself.

## SURVEYING PROCEDURE

There are three main methods of surveying – running dimension, offsets, and triangulation, but it is best to begin by drawing an overall sketch plan of the site, on which all major features are noted. Spend some time investigating the site, walking around the boundary to familiarize yourself with the layout. Then return to the house to work out the procedure to be used on the particular site. It is usually easiest to start with the house and with elements close to the house, typically within a 5-metre (5-yard) range, before measuring more distant elements, such as boundaries and trees.

### Taking the measurements

You will use a combination of your short and long tapes to measure the site. The rigid metal tape is straightforward to use and requires no explanation. The long tape, however, needs more careful handling. The easiest and most efficient way of using it is to keep the tape measure under your left arm (or right arm if you are left-handed) and to pay out or gather in the tape using your right hand. Between dimensions, treat the loose tape as if it were a coil of rope, looping it over your arm. Wind in the tape only when you have completed surveying an area. When you wind in the tape, do so through a damp rag or cloth, otherwise dirt will get into the case and the tape may jam.

*Using a sheet of graph paper, begin your survey by drawing the house and other close features.*

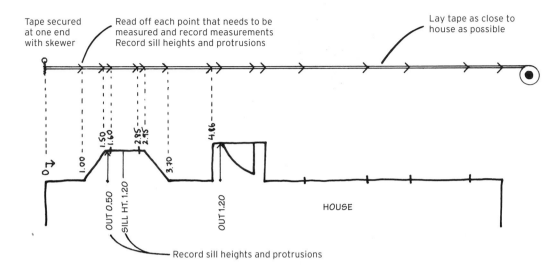

Tape secured at one end with skewer

Read off each point that needs to be measured and record measurements Record sill heights and protrusions

Lay tape as close to house as possible

OUT 0.50
SILL HT. 1.20
OUT 1.20

HOUSE

Record sill heights and protrusions

**Measuring the house and nearby elements**
Sketch an outline plan of the house on a sheet of graph paper. Make it as large as possible but leave some room for writing in measurements around the side. Using graph paper helps to keep the proportions and relative positions of elements in the drawing reasonably correct, but do not attempt to draw the site to scale, unless it is very tiny, as this is too time-consuming.

While you are doing this, note the position of windows and doors, and direction of opening, and any elements close to the house, such as drains, manhole covers or nearby shrubs. If the site is a very small one you could include the boundaries and all existing garden elements on this first sheet of paper, but it is usually best to avoid cluttering one diagram unnecessarily and resketching the house outline for another plan can be done in a very short time.

*Above: Measure each side of the house using running, or progressive, measurements.*

*Below: Using long and short tapes, take right-angle offsets to locate individual items close to the house.*

You are now ready to start measuring each side of the house. Pay out your tape along the length of the house, as close to the house wall as possible. Then lay the reel down on the ground and go back to the beginning of your tape. This should line up with one corner of the house and be secured with a metal skewer or brick to ensure that it does not move. The tape must be taut and untwisted along its length before you start to read off any measurements.

Now, starting at the beginning of your tape, read off the position of all edges, doors, windows, taps, drains and so on along the house wall. This method of measuring, which is called taking **running or baseline measurements** is quicker and much more accurate than taking measurements by shifting the tape along. Mark the beginning point with O and an arrow to show the direction in which you are measuring.

Try to record all subsequent baselines measurements with the figures orientated in the same direction. This should help minimize the risk of confusing them with other measurements when you are drawing up the plan later.

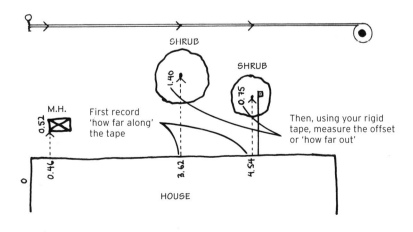

SHRUB

SHRUB

M.H.

First record 'how far along' the tape

Then, using your rigid tape, measure the offset or 'how far out'

HOUSE

When you have recorded all the horizontal measurements, use your rigid tape to take down measurements of the heights of window sills, lights, taps and so on and of any indents of protuberances of the building. These measurements can be taken quite quickly by establishing a common base line as a datum, such as the horizontal damp-proof course.

You can also measure elements close to the house by using a combination of your long and short tapes. With your tape still running along the house wall, not how far along an element occurs, and then, using your short tape, note how far out it is form the house wall. This method of is called **offset measuring**.

## Measuring more distant elements

When you have completed the house survey, take a fresh piece of graph paper and sketch on it the sit boundary. Within this, draw in the house and any other elements that you wish to locate, such as trees, paths and garages. To ascertain their exact positions, you will be using a system of measuring called **triangulation**, which is used to locate a third point in relation to two know points or an established baseline. You can, for instance, ascertain the position of a tree by using as reference points two corners of the house that you have already measured. Simply measure and note down the distance from each corner to the tree. Back in your office, you can plot the measurements using a compass, as shown in the diagram.

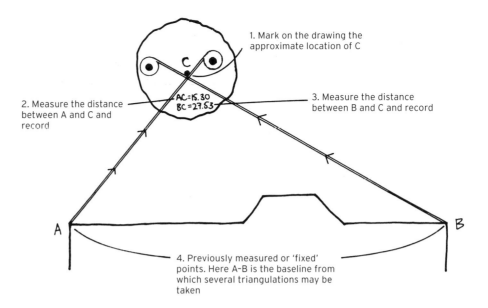

1. Mark on the drawing the approximate location of C

2. Measure the distance between A and C and record

3. Measure the distance between B and C and record

AC=15.30
BC=27.53

4. Previously measured or 'fixed' points. Here A–B is the baseline from which several triangulations may be taken

*From two fixed points A and B, use triangulation to locate distant elements, such as point C. Back in the studio a scaled drawing can then be produced from the measurements taken.*

Back in the studio

Arc BC

The point at which the arcs cross is the location of C

Arc AC

15.30m (yd)

27.53m (yd)

2. Place the compass point here to draw arc AC

1. Draw the baseline at the chosen scale

3. Place the compass point here to draw arc BC

*After drawing in the house, boundaries and other site elements, use capital letters to label the main corners of the house and all other relevant points to be measured.*

Before you start to measure it is often helpful to label on your sketch all the points that will need to be located and the known points rom which they will be triangulated. Triangulation is very useful for establishing elements that are not parallel or at right angles to a building, such as paths or boundaries. Often they may appear to be so, but triangulating the points reveals otherwise! When you choose a baseline or two fixed points from which to measure, try to select the longest unobstructed line, from which all or most of the area can be seen. For most sites, however, particularly when the house is surrounded by the garden, you will need more than one baseline.

What appears to look like this

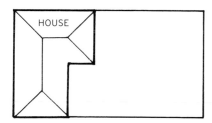

may, in reality, be this shape

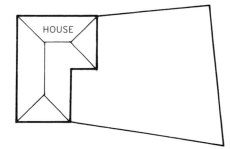

*Above: Always use triangulation to measure boundaries.*

When you are recording your measurements you may like to write the distances down next to the point you are trying to establish, or at the side of your drawing. If you first make a note of all the measurements you will have to take, you will reduce the risk of

*Right: To prevent your drawing from becoming cluttered and illegible, record all the elements as neatly as possible. Figures can be recorded either close to the relevant point on the sketch or at the side of the drawing.*

leaving the site without having completed your measuring.

If the distances to be measured are longer than your 30m (100ft) tape, you can use a ball of string to set out the line first. The measuring can then be tackled in stages. You may find it

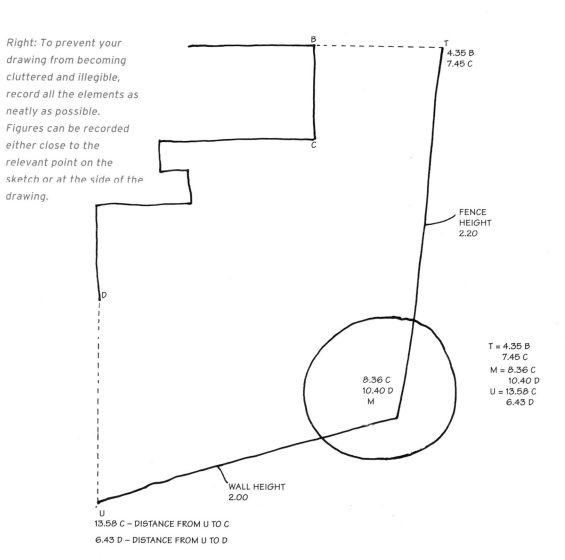

13.58 C – DISTANCE FROM U TO C

6.43 D – DISTANCE FROM U TO D

helpful to use garden canes or other markers placed at regular intervals, which can later be totalled up.

### Measuring curves

Curves, such as curving paths, bed or boundaries are measured using offsets, taken at regular intervals from a baseline or a triangulation line. When taking an offset measurement you must ensure that it is taken at 90° to your baseline. You may find it useful to use a rectangular object, such as a piece of cardboard, to make the right angle.

## OTHER METHODS OF MEASURING

### The clock method for surveying small gardens

This technique is especially useful for small, fairly cluttered gardens, in which objects may obstruct the view from one corner of the plot to another. In this case, the baseline is formed by two garden canes, placed centrally, but some distance apart in the garden. Starting at one corner of the house, walk around the garden in a clockwise direction labelling every point that you wish to measure, ending up with the garden canes themselves. At the side of your drawing list all the distances from each of these points to the first cane, and then from each of these points to the second cane, not forgetting to note the distance between the two canes. Securing the end of your tape measure to the first cane you can now quickly rotate around the garden recording all the measurements, and then do the same from your second cane.

*Right: Use a combination of triangulation and offsets to measure a curved path.*

*Below: In the systematic clock method of surveying measurements can be taken and recorded quickly.*

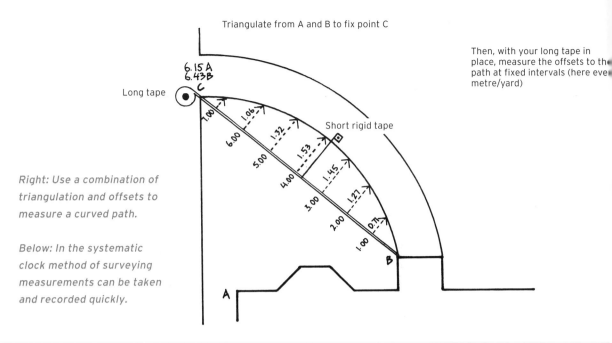

Triangulate from A and B to fix point C

Then, with your long tape in place, measure the offsets to the path at fixed intervals (here every metre/yard)

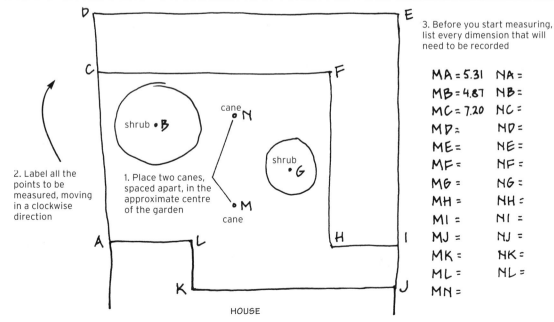

2. Label all the points to be measured, moving in a clockwise direction

1. Place two canes, spaced apart, in the approximate centre of the garden

3. Before you start measuring, list every dimension that will need to be recorded

| | |
|---|---|
| MA = 5.31 | NA = |
| MB = 4.87 | NB = |
| MC = 7.20 | NC = |
| MD = | ND = |
| ME = | NE = |
| MF = | NF = |
| MG = | NG = |
| MH = | NH = |
| MI = | NI = |
| MJ = | NJ = |
| MK = | NK = |
| ML = | NL = |
| MN = | |

HOUSE

## Measuring slopes or changes in level

Few sites are absolutely flat, and it is beyond the scope of this book to explain how to take levels using a theodolite and staff. However, it is possible to work out simple levels by using a spirit level, pegs and a plank. Start at the top of a slope and choose some level, permanent feature, such as a manhole cover, low retaining wall or step, and measure out from it a distance rather less than the length of the plank. At that point, drive in a peg so that its top is approximately level with the height of the permanent feature. Place the plank on the peg and rest a spirit level on it. You may need to adjust the peg until the spirit level shows a true level reading. Then measure the vertical distance between the plank and the slope.

Alternatively, simply squat down beside some permanent feature, such as a low wall, and compare by eye how much the ground, or any object rises or falls over a given distance. This will enable you to estimate the gradients. Counting the number of brick courses can also be helpful as a check on heights.

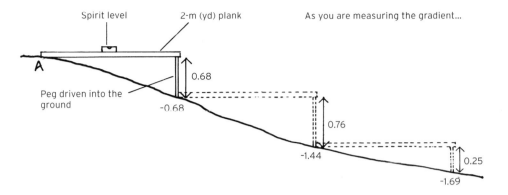

Spirit level | 2-m (yd) plank | As you are measuring the gradient...

Peg driven into the ground

0.68
−0.68
0.76
−1.44
0.25
−1.69

... record the progressive measurements on your sketch

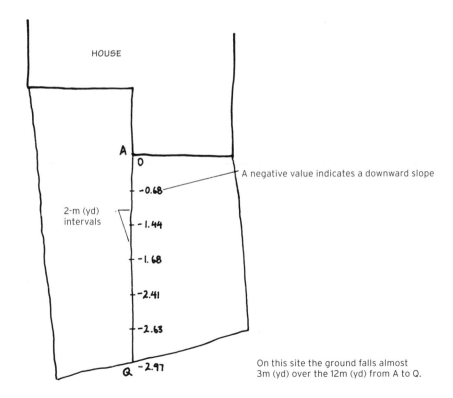

HOUSE

A
0

A negative value indicates a downward slope

−0.68

2-m (yd) intervals

−1.44

−1.68

−2.41

−2.63

Q −2.97

On this site the ground falls almost 3m (yd) over the 12m (yd) from A to Q.

*Right: Use a 2-m (yd) plank, spirit level and pegs to measure a slope.*

### Measuring trees or large shrubs

In addition to naming each tree, there are five measurements that may need to be recorded:

- the centre of the trunk
- the diameter (or girth) of the trunk
- the width or spread of the tree canopy
- the height of the lowest branches
- the overall height of the tree

Having located the centre of the trunk by the triangulation or offset method, both the diameter or girth and the canopy spread can be estimated by using a tape laid on the ground. To estimate the height of the lowest branch and the overall tree height, it is useful to have an assistant. Ask him or her to stand by the tree and work out, using your assistant's height as a guide, how many times the height goes into the lower branches and the overall height. If you do not have an assistant, find some other object with a known height, such as a garden building, and work out the height from that reference point. Mark in these dimensions alongside the centre of the tree.

*Below: Use the height of a person as a reference to estimate the height of trees.*

Approximately 6m (yd)

Approximately 2m (yd)

Approximately 4m (yd)

## SOIL TYPE OR PH FACTOR

The existing vegetation may give you a clear indication of the soil type. Some plants, such as rhododendrons, camellias, heathers and other ericaceous plants, prefer acid soil or soil that is low in lime, nitrogen and phosphate, but in which minerals such as manganese are available to the plant. Acid soil, which is rich in ion, often occurs in rural areas that are, or were, heavily wooded, and where leaves and other debris have, over the centuries, created a thick layer of decomposing material, which has interacted with soil and subsoil to produce damp, peaty conditions.

Alkaline soil is unable to provide iron, manganese and boron in a universally acceptable form, and plants that require these minerals are unable to exist in these conditions.

The acidity or alkalinity of the soil is measured on a pH scale, which varies from pH1, very acid to pH14, very alkaline. Plants vary in their degree of tolerance to high and low pH, and although most will grow on soil that is close to neutral (pH7), an indication of the soil type must be established before any serious planting can begin. It is always wise to test the soil, and you will need to collect a small amount from a range of points representative of the overall site. You may find the soil differs in various parts of the garden.

To do this you will need a trowel, small polythene bags, labels and a pen. Decide at which points the soil should be taken – under trees, in open ground, at the base of walls, for example – and mark these points as SS1 (soil sample 1), SS2 and so on on the survey. Use the trowel to take about a tablespoonful of soil from approximately 100mm (4in) below the surface, tip it into a polythene bag, label the bag and tie it securely. When you get back to your office, tip the soil onto saucers and place each one on top of the now empty, labelled bag, and allow it to dry out naturally before testing with a soil-testing kit. Alternatively, send the samples to a soil-testing laboratory. The findings will later be recorded in the analysis of the site.

While you are taking samples for pH purposes, you will also need to consider the soil texture – the relative proportions of sand, silt and clay that the soil contains.

A less messy, but less accurate, method of testing soil is to use a soil meter, which can be pushed into the ground to give an immediate reading.

### Some useful soil indicators
- Viburnum/spindle – chalky; alkaline soil
- Heather or ling – dry; acid or peaty soil
- Nettle/ chickweed – potentially fertile soil
- Sheep's sorrel – poor, light, dry, acid soil
- Foxgloves – dry, sandy or gravely soil
- Furze, gorse or broom – poor, infertile soil

SS1 – SANDY  SS2 – VERY DRY  SS3 – SLIGHTLY WATERLOGGED

## RECORDING NON-MEASURABLE DETAILS

You will now have written down many measurements, but before you return to your office or studio, there are many non-measurable factors to be taken into account.

A garden cannot be looked at in isolation – it must be considered in the context of its surroundings, and every site, however small or confined, is in reality a part of some larger whole with which it interacts, affecting and being affected by this wider environment.

Some of these factors may be visual, such as views within the garden, from the house, terrace or other vantage points, lawns or the architectural style of the house or even architectural details, like existing wall copings, which may be incorporated into a new wall design, or they may be to do with the climate or even the character, sound and smell of the site. The qualitative characteristics of existing features, such as the materials from which they are made, should also be noted – a brick wall which is in need of repair, for example.

In addition to revealing what lies within the boundaries, the survey must examine what lies beyond. This is called the **zone of visual influence**, and it may extend no further than the backs of houses in the next street or it may reach to a stretch of public footpath on a distant hillside. However near or far, the zone must be defined before any real consideration can be given to design. Certain rooms within

*Left: When taking soil samples (SS), note their location and number the samples accordingly. Also note the condition and texture of the soil.*

the house may give distant views, and you should stand at the windows and do a quick sketch or take a photograph of what you can see. Select vantage points outside the house – a terrace or some sunny area where the client may wish to sit, for instance – and do another quick sketch. Only outline shapes are necessary and speed is important, for you will often be surveying in bad weather with fading light.

## Orientation

All plans for the garden should take into account how the position of the sun affects the garden. Unless the weather is really bad, you can easily do this by looking to see the position of the sun at the time of your visit and working out where it will be at noon. Usually the owners of the garden will also be able to tell you, but you can check the exact orientation by using a compass or looking at a street plan or map.

When you draw a plan you should always indicate the north point. Remember, too, that the amount of sun or shade that a garden receives will vary – in winter the arc of the sun is lower, making shadows wider and deeper, while in summer, although the sun is higher, deciduous trees in full leaf can cast shade.

## Climate

The climate will affect the way in which the garden is designed and used. The site location, aspect, altitude, topography and temperature will all have a bearing on the site, and should be noted at this stage – a seaside garden will be affected by wind and salt spray, for example, which will mean that only plants tolerant of these conditions can be used.

*Right: This plan shows how the location of the sun at different times of the day can alter the areas of shade in a garden.*

*Below: This diagram shows the areas of summer and winter shade in a north-facing garden.*

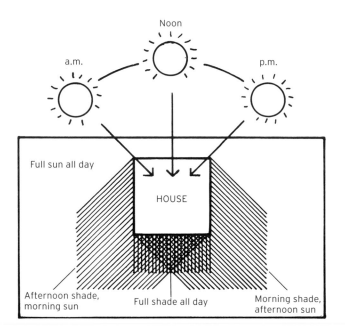

Noon

a.m.                                p.m.

Full sun all day

HOUSE

Afternoon shade, morning sun        Full shade all day        Morning shade, afternoon sun

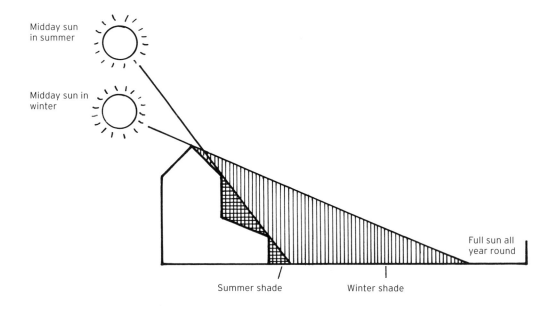

Midday sun in summer

Midday sun in winter

Full sun all year round

Summer shade        Winter shade

The direction of the wind can also render certain parts of the garden unusable. This may not be apparent on your particular visit, so you should ask the client or find out from a local weather station or airport. In some situations, wind speeds can be increased by being 'funnelled' between high buildings, while obstructions can direct the wind, causing it to blow from unexpected quarters.

You should also be aware of the possible existence of a microclimate within a garden. The climatic conditions within particular defined spaces can vary considerably from the average local climate. For instance, if a garden is on a windy hillside but is surrounded by high walls, the area immediately in the lee of these walls will be sheltered, but the more open space beyond will still be subject to wind.

## SITE INVENTORY

Every site will have its own limitations, which will affect design proposals. Go through a site inventory before you leave the site. Some of the points will not be relevant while others that are not on the list may be raised, but all the information must be noted down while you are on site and transferred to a site analysis at a later stage.

*A typical checklist of site conditions.*

---

## SITE INVENTORY

Client name: _____

Client address: _____

Work to be undertaken: _____

_____

### 1. General

Date and time of site survey: _____

Weather conditions: _____

Did weather conditions prevent any of the site being accessed    Yes/No

If yes, explain _____

Site photographed?  Yes/No

Orientation determined?  Yes/No

Soil sample taken?  Yes/No

### 2. The house

Style and age of property: _____

Condition: _____

Building materials: _____

Is the property in a conservation area?  Yes/No

Locations of doors and windows: _____

Are any doors/windows emergency exits?    Yes/No

If so, which? _____

Downpipes:    Shown on site survey: Yes/No

Exterior lights:    Shown on site survey: Yes/No

Electricity meter: Shown on site survey: Yes/No                    cont.

Gas meter:      Shown on site survey: Yes/No

Outside taps:  Shown on site survey: Yes/No

Dustbins:        Shown on site survey: Yes/No

Washing line:  Shown on site survey: Yes/No

Drainage channels: Shown on site survey: Yes/No

Has cabling for telephones or cable TV been laid recently?

If so, where?   Are cables close to soil surface?   Yes/No

Will this present problems for contractors?   Yes/No


**3. What surrounds the property?**

Front boundary: _____

Right-hand boundary: _____

Left-hand boundary: _____

Rear boundary: _____

Nearby traffic levels: _____

High? Medium? Low?

Noise intrusion on property: _____

High? Medium? Low?

Are noise intrusions detailed on site survey?   Yes/No

Does the site smell?   Yes/No  If yes, detail: _____

Access from street/road: _____

Pedestrian Yes/No

Vehicular Yes/No

Both Yes/No?

Explain: _____

Is the site overlooked? Yes/No If yes, explain: _____

**4. Garden construction**

What hard landscaping materials have been used in the garden?

Paths         Retain? Yes/No

Steps         Retain? Yes/No


Walls/Fences            Retain? Yes/No

Other structures        Retain? Yes/No


**5. Climate**

General feel of the garden: _____

Prevailing wind: _____

Have sunny and shady areas been marked on site survey? Yes/No


**6. Condition of site:**

Are there signs of soil erosion?   Yes/No

Poor drainage?          Yes/No

Depth of soil (if determinable) _____

Have changes of level been marked on site survey? Yes/No


**7. Planting**

What plants can remain?_____

What plants can be removed? _____

Condition of trees      Good/Bad

If bad, explain: _____

Action to be taken: _____

Are any trees protected by TPOs? Yes/No (mark on site survey)

Any other considerations? _____

## USING A CAMERA TO RECORD DATA

A camera is an invaluable tool for recording site information. Often there is so much information to be noted that the naked eye, however well trained, overlooks some detail – an ugly light fitting, overhead telephone cables, the condition or state of existing walls – and even obvious lines and shapes may not have appeared apparent while you were on site. Such features will be revealed on a photograph, to be studied carefully when back in your studio.

### Reasons for site photography
Photographic prints can be used as:
• a reminder of the site
• as a basis for a report on the existing garden
• as a basis for quick overlays or sketches to show how the garden might look if replanned
• as a record of the garden before during, and after replanning and planting
• as a portfolio to of projects to show future clients
• as a record of seasonal or growth changes as the garden develops

### Old photographs
• can indicate the historical background or previous use of the site

### Aerial photographs
• can reveal previous ground patterns, or the outlines of former planted beds, useful in restoration projects

### Types of photographs
The main categories of photograph that will be required are:
• panoramic vies from the house
• views of, and back to, the house from the far end or boundary of the garden
• close-ups of specific items and their condition – terraces, walls, pergola, conservatory, existing planting and so on.

Using the methods outlined below will enable you to have a complete photographic record of the site. When they have been developed the prints should be clearly labelled with the client's name and address and the date on which they were taken. They can be filed or mounted above your desk or drawing board for future reference.

**Panoramic shots** Begin with panoramic views from the house. Choose a central position – often a doorway – and standing with your back to the house and using your body as a pivot shoot first to the far left-hand side, while carefully noting what is in the far right-hand side of the picture frame. Take the second shot by just including in the left-hand side of the frame what was seen in the right-hand side of the previous frame. Continue by moving around clockwise in a half-circle or circle, keeping the camera as steady and level as possible – a tripod will help – until you have completed the panoramic view. Occasionally it may be necessary to take a near, middle and distant panorama to show plantings, buildings and boundaries in sufficient detail.

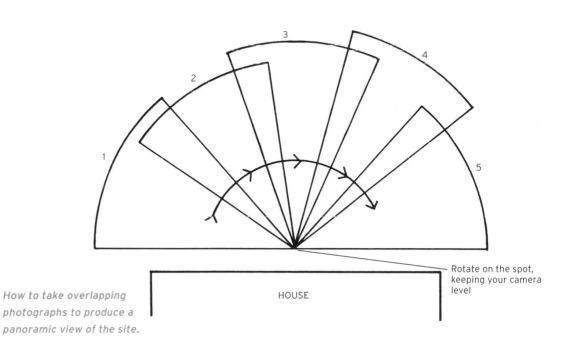

*How to take overlapping photographs to produce a panoramic view of the site.*

HOUSE

Rotate on the spot, keeping your camera level

**Views of the house** Next move to the opposite end of the area or to an imaginary line some distance from the house to take the views of, and back to, the house. Set up this imaginary 'line' and move along it from left to right, again using the 'overlap' system.

This method will give you a 'flat' view of the house or building, which as well as being a useful basis for an overlay or sketch of that the house and garden may look like after replanning, will also provide a record of the position of doors, windows, downpipes and so on. If the site is very large, it will need to be sub-divided into different areas, similar to the measured areas for the survey, each of which will be treated separately.

The best views of a small garden and its surroundings are often captured by photo-graphing from an upstairs window. This will enable you to look down onto the site and to include adjacent gardens, houses or other buildings. The scene will alter from summer to winter – a sycamore tree that is in leaf and casting heavy shade on the garden may be hiding the view of an unsightly factory or handsome church spire, while in winter, when the tree is bare, the garden may appear sunny and light but be overlooked.

**Close-ups of existing features** Finally, walk round the site and take close-ups of anything you particularly want to record. These may be a severe crack in a wall, poor drainage on a terrace or a badly shaped tree. Often the reason for your photograph will be to point out to the client the need for repair or removal!

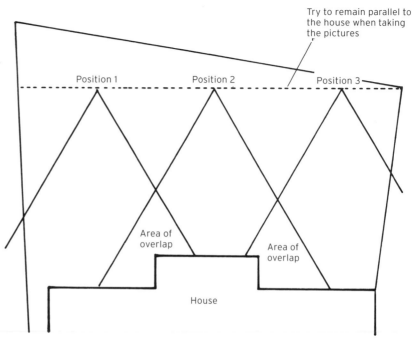

*Right: The technique used to take photographs from the house and views back to it. These are useful as a record and as the basis for overlays.*

Try to remain parallel to the house when taking the pictures

Position 1    Position 2    Position 3

Area of overlap    Area of overlap

House

**Aerial photographs** If the site being worked on is of particular historical significance, it may be useful to obtain or commission aerial photographs of the site. These are best taken in dry weather because previous groundworks will show more clearly in drought. There are a number of specialist firms that have picture libraries or that can arrange the photography for you. Occasionally pictorial records may be obtained from magazines or research libraries.

**Uses of photographs** If you intend to publish articles or books you may need photographs to accompany text, and publishers require colour transparencies, rather than prints. You may, therefore, wish to take additional photographs for this purpose. Alternatively, you may simply want to keep a photographic record of the

gardens as they develop. It is always interesting to compare 'before' with 'after', and it is an effective way of impressing future clients.

Once the photographs have been taken and the film developed, you can decide how best to use them. If you are using the 'panorama' method, the photographs should be overlapped, stuck down and mounted on to card to fix on a wall above your drawing board for easy reference. If they are to be used in a report or for sketching over, some views can be selected and duplicates made. If necessary, the photograph can be enlarged to a suitable size on a photocopier and then sketched over using tracing paper. Photographs can also be stuck round the site inventory and analysis sheet to clarify certain comments.

*Use your body as a pivot to take overlapping shots from left to right. This will give you a 'flat' view to refer to later.*

*Photographs are an excellent method of recording the good and less good features of any site.*

# CHAPTER FOUR

# Drawing up the site plan

The survey must now be drawn up to scale. This drawing will become the base plan and, because future design work will be carried out by tracing over it, it must be an accurate representation of the site. Even if the site is an awkward shape, the outline drawing should fit comfortably on a standard size sheet of paper, with enough space for additional notes or drawings. The outline must also be sufficiently distinct to be visible through several sheets of tracing paper.

## SETTING UP THE EQUIPMENT

Before you can begin any drawing you will need to set up a work place. This should be equipped with an anglepoise lamp, set to shine from left to right if you are right-handed, and the drawing equipment listed in Chapter 1.

Make sure that your drawing board is set at a comfortable angle and that your parallel motion is parallel to the base of your board. Begin by securing a backing sheet of gridded graph paper to the drawing board with masking tape, checking that the horizontal lines on the sheet correspond to the parallel motion. Similarly, check by using a set-square, held firmly against your parallel motion, that the vertical lines also correspond. Once it is stuck down, the backing paper will serve for months as a guide to setting up a drawing, for lettering and for general layout, so it must be positioned correctly. The chosen size of tracing paper should be positioned on top of this and also secured with masking tape at the corners. The survey notes can now be drawn to scale on this sheet.

## CHOOSING THE SCALE

The purpose of a scale drawing is to produce an accurate representation of the garden on paper, with everything shown in its correct position. This scale drawing will act as a basis for all the following steps in the design process. In reality the garden is rarely seen

Graph paper

Masking tape

Orientate the strips of tape this way to prevent cut ends catching on the parallel motion

Use a set square to check that vertical lines are straight

Use the parallel motion to check that horizontal lines are straight

*Securing the graph paper backing sheet to the drawing board.*

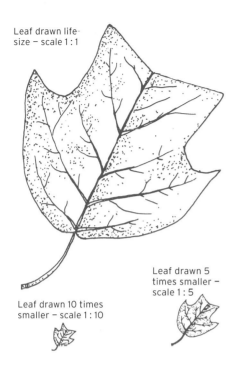

Leaf drawn 5 times smaller – scale 1 : 5

Leaf drawn 10 times smaller – scale 1 : 10

*A tulip tree leaf drawn to scale.*

from this 'overhead' view, unless from an aeroplane, but it is necessary to work on a plan so that one can see at a glance how each object or space relates to another. Because a successful garden design relies heavily on the relationship of one area to another, an accurate plan must be the basis for future design work.

On any scale rule you will find series of ratios – 1 : 1, 1 : 10, 1 : 20, 1 : 50, 1 : 100, 1 : 200 and so on – representing different scales. The largest scale is 1 : 1, which represents a reproduction of the same size as the original. If the drawing is reproduced at 1 : 10, it will be 10 times smaller.

In garden design the most common scales are 1 : 50, 1 : 100 and 1 : 200, which are used for both garden layout plans and planting plans.

Detailing is generally drawn to scales of 1 : 5, 1 : 10, 1 : 20 or 1 : 50. Cartographic maps are usually drawn to scales of 1 : 1250 and 1 : 2500, and they are really only of use in garden design in determining points such as the orientation and precise location of a site.

Drawing the survey up to scale is always an exciting task, and it should always be done as quickly as possible after the site visit, as notes are always easier to read while they are still fresh in the mind.

Sometimes, when you are plotting the measurements, it becomes obvious that a

dimension has either been noted down incorrectly or has been overlooked entirely. If it is discovered immediately, the client can be asked to check the vital dimension or the site can be revisited. This is less easy if the mistake is found only three weeks later and two days before the plan is due to be finished.

The survey can be drawn up on various sizes of paper, but to produce a professional design from which printed copies can be made the final layout plan will need to be drawn on tracing paper, which is normally available in standard sizes, ranging from A4 (11²⁄₃ x 8¹⁄₄in) to A0 (46³⁄₄ x 33¹⁄₈in). Most gardens will be drawn up on A2 (23¹⁄₂ x 16¹⁄₂in) paper, but if the garden is large or if a lot of detail, such as

A quick sketch of the site drawn to a scale of 1 : 100

Overall length

Overall width

HOUSE

Survey only just fits onto an A2 (23¹⁄₃ x 16¹⁄₂in) sheet, leaving inadequate space for labels and notes

HOUSE

Or reduce the scale

Survey fits comfortably onto an A2 (23¹⁄₂ x 16¹⁄₂ in) sheet at 1 : 200

Either go up a paper size

NOTES

Survey fits comfortably onto an A1 (33¹⁄₈ x 23¹⁄₂ in) sheet at 1 : 100

*Paper size and the scale to be used for drawing up the survey need to be considered together.*

paving steps or intricate planting, is to be shown it may be better to work to a larger scale on a larger sheet such as A1 (33⅛ x 23½in). If the garden is an awkward shape, the outline may need to be moved around before it will fit on the sheet. It is also easier and less expensive to reproduce smaller sheet sizes. Although there is much work to be done before you can commit yourself to your final paper size, there is little point in drawing up the survey to scale, only to have to enlarge or reduce it later.

Begin by measuring and drawing to scale the overall length of the garden and then its overall width. Will these overall dimensions fit comfortably onto your intended sheet size, or will the site plan take up all the available space or appear too large or too small? When you choose a scale or size of paper try to find a balance, making sure that you fit all necessary details without having to draw up a huge plan.

## DRAWING THE SITE PLAN

When you have selected the scale to fit the chosen size of tracing paper, or vice versa, the survey measurements and notes can be plotted on the tracing paper to make an accurate survey drawn to scale or a site plan. Even though this survey will mainly be used as a basis for later drawings, it should still be placed centrally on the sheet, with space left for notes around it.

When you draw up the site plan it is logical to proceed in exactly the same order as you surveyed the site, beginning with the base line of the house and working out from that until the boundaries have been completed. In trying to decide which way to place the survey, it may help to think of the client's main viewing points

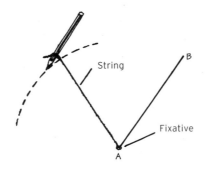

*If a dimension is longer than the stretch of your compass, use a piece of string with a pencil attached to make the arc.*

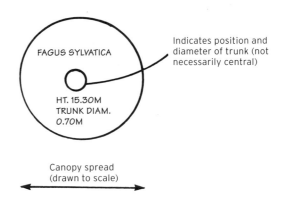

*How to show existing trees on a plan.*

of the garden and to set the plan at a similar angle. When drawing, always use a very sharp pencil or clutch pencil, because blunt leads can give inaccurate dimensions. Try not to smudge the graphite by working over it with your hand. Use a duster or drawing board brush to keep your work clean and free from eraser rubbings.

### Where to begin

Begin by drawing the house at the chosen scale and then use compasses to locate the boundary, a tree or another building. In many cases the distance measured will be longer than the stretch of the extension arm and therefore difficult to locate accurately, but it can be achieved by using a combination of scale rule, string and pencil – perhaps a slightly Heath Robinson approach, but nevertheless effective. You may wish to use a beam compass, but this is quite an expensive item.

Continue moving round the site on paper as on the actual site until all measurements have been transposed. Tick off each dimension as it is plotted as a check on what has already been done. In some cases, an absolutely accurate

rendering may not be easy – points may not quite join up, for example – and therefore a little artistic licence may be allowed. However, if the dimensions do not meet, or are seriously out, it may be wise to revisit the site to check them.

### Plotting trees and other items

When you are plotting trees, show the actual position of the trunk and the spread of the canopy, including a note of the overall height and if, known, the botanical and common names. Shrubs or other plants that may play a significant part in the new design should similarly be indicated. The heights and thickness of walls, measurements of the treads and risers of steps and the overall dimensions of any other relevant artefacts should also be shown, as should manhole covers, septic tanks and if known, the drainage system and the level of the damp-proof course (DPC). Problems arising from the location of these items may affect the design, and although they can be talked through on site with the contractor, there is no point in disregarding their whereabouts at this early stage.

FREE-STANDING WALL
1.65M

RETAINING WALL
0.45M

Note that a thinner
line is used for the
inside of the retaining
walls

*How to indicate walls on a plan, giving information on height and width.*

The first pencil-drawn survey is often fairly messy, the sheet being punctured with arcs and pin pricks from your compasses, and it may need to be retraced to make it more legible. Take a further sheet of tracing paper, stick it down over the drawn survey and trace over it in pencil or, preferably, ink because this is darker and easier to read through several sheets of paper as the design is being worked up.

### North point, scale and your address
Finally, in the bottom right-hand corner, insert the north point, the scale at which the survey has been drawn, the address of the property and the date on which the drawing was finished. Note that putting both the name and address of the client has not been suggested, so that some degree of anonymity can be preserved. Your name, address and telephone number should also be included on the plan.

This drawing will now become the site plan, from which the new garden layout will emerge. It will show the existing elements on site and will be used as a basis for the site analysis. For this reason it is occasionally also referred to as a base plan, but the term site plan is now more commonly used.

*A professional site survey, showing spot heights.*

# CHAPTER FIVE

# The site inventory and site analysis

The site inventory and site analysis are two interim stages between drawing up the site plan and beginning the design. These drawings are very rarely seen by the client, but they are a means by which the garden designer gains an understanding of the problems and potential of a particular site.

## WHY A SITE INVENTORY AND ANALYSIS ARE NEEDED

For various reasons, the design or construction work cannot always begin immediately, and the inventory is a factual description of the state of the site at the time of the survey, to which you will refer frequently when you are initially planning the new design. Usually the constraints and limitations of a site outweigh the advantages, but both must be taken into account..

Sometimes a client may wish to alter or revise a particular aspect of the completed garden layout plan, contrary to the designer's advice. Referring back to the inventory and analysis will serve to jog your memory and remind you of your reasons for deciding on a particular design and enable you to explain your motives for handling the project in a particular way.

### How to prepare them

The simplest way to prepare the inventory and analysis is on two separate drawings, which can be made as tracing paper overlays o the site or base plan. Alternatively, you could use a copy negative of the base plan to save any redrawing (see page 125). The first drawing, the inventory, is an accurate factual account of the current state of everything within, and immediately without, the site, and it should be compiled from the notes taken on the survey visit – 'boundary wall in poor condition, brick coping deteriorating', 'lawn mostly moss/little grass evident' or 'old pear tree showing dieback/disease on some branches', for example. Positive features, too, should be included – 'fine views to distant hills', for example – until all features within the garden have received comment. Remember to include the immediate surroundings, and notes taken on site may reveal comments such as 'distant view partially obscured by overgrown sycamore'.

### Using graphic symbols

Whenever information can be most simply expressed as graphic symbols, use them to help bring the plans to life. You may, for instance, like to use blue hatching to denote damp or windy, exposed areas or yellow stars for sunny, warm areas.

### Analysis and illustrating the information

The second sheet, the site analysis, should evaluate the importance of the information on the inventory by looking at ways of solving the problems and by taking advantage of the potential offered by existing site conditions – 'remove overgrown sycamore to reveal distant view' or 'plant hedges to obscure view of neighbour's shed', for example. Although these drawings will not generally be seen by the client, there are occasions when plans have to be put before a committee, which may require a clear, simple proposal to help it reach a decision. In this case it is best to have the site inventory and analysis complete with notes printed or photocopied and then to add colour for emphasis and clarity. The removal of trees, for instance, is always an emotive subject, and those trees under threat can be circled in red to show their precise location and so facilitate an informed discussion of the reasons behind the proposed removal. With practice and

*A site inventory provides a record of existing features and the state of the site.*

LARCH LAP FENCING IN POOR STATE

COLD NORTH-EASTERLY WIND

ENTRANCE TOO NARROW

VIEW OF PASSING CARS

GARAGE

BEDS VERY BARE IN WINTER

DRIVE TOO DOMINANT

SUNNY

POOL

WOODLAND TREES – SADLY DEPLETED AFTER RECENT STORM

SUMMER HOUSE

UGLY BARE WALL

HOUSE

PROVIDE SEATING IN POOL VICINITY

BARN

NOISY ROAD

ENTRANCE TO WOODS UNINTERESTING

SWING (FIXED)

UNEVEN LAWN

SUNNY AREA

POOL AREA OVERLOOKED BY NEIGHBOURS

PATIO OVERLOOKED FROM NEIGHBOUR'S BEDROOM

**SITE INVENTORY FOR A SMALLER GARDEN**

*This analysis suggests ways of improving the site.*

PLANT MORE TREES – ORNAMENTAL FORMS OF NATIVE TREES

REPLACE OLD FENCING

GOOD SITE FOR BENCH

EMPHASIZE VISTA TO OAK FROM NEIGHBOURING FIELD

PLANT TREES AS WINDBREAK, TO MUFFLE TRAFFIC NOISE AND TO SCREEN VIEW OF ROAD

GARAGE

IMPORTANT VIEW – REMOVE OBSTRUCTING TREES

POOL

MORE EVERGREEN PLANTS

CLOSE AND REDIRECT DRIVE

WIDEN ENTRANCE

PLANT HERE TO IMPROVE VIEW FROM BARN

SCREEN VIEW OF POOL FROM HOUSE

EMPHASIZE THIS ENTRANCE

HOUSE

PROVIDE ACCESS

SUMMER HOUSE

INTEGRATE SWING INTO NEW DESIGN

BARN

MAINTAIN OPEN LAWN, BUT LEVEL

REDUCE WIDTH OF ENTRANCE TO CREATE ATMOSPHERE OF SECRECY

CREATE TERRACE FOR EVENING USE

SITE ANALYSIS

SCREEN VIEW OF NEIGHBOURS

SCREEN VIEW OF NEIGHBOURS HOUSE

imagination, the site inventory and analysis can become an informative and colourful document that provides a summary of the requirements and, to some extent, the intent of the design. The inventory and analysis can also accompany a report.

## WRITING A REPORT

A report is often the final step in the research and preparation phase. It is seldom necessary for a small garden, but for a larger garden it is an invaluable method of summarizing the state of the existing garden, making proposals for improvements and providing the basis for future design work. It is a useful way of beginning a large and lengthy project, and it should contain enough information for constructive discussion and to help the client and designer decide how and when to proceed within implementing the plan.

The report should be compiled in the same way as the site analysis and appraisal, but, because it is normally used for larger gardens, estates or commercial developments, it is easier to break the site down into different areas and to comment on each particular area, possibly discussing in each case such items as paving, paths, steps and walls, tree planting and decorative planting. Often, for ease of referral, a report will need to be accompanied by a scale survey of the entire site, with each area divided up to correspond with the areas in the report.

Photographs can be used to illustrate some points, and the photographic method of illustration can be taken further by doing a tracing paper sketch as an overlay – a quick and easy 'before' and 'after'. If the 'after' is drawn carefully in ink it can then be printed on a clear acetate or left on tracing paper to give a clear, impressive, yet simple way of illustrating, for instance, how the view will alter after the removal of the sycamore tree.

It is important not to give away too many design ideas at the report stage, or clients may try to implement them themselves. A report should entice your clients into employing you. It can also be used to explain the motives behind a design to associated professionals, such as architects working on a hotel complex or other large-scale work, and copies of it can easily be made to give to the various people concerned in such a development.

*A sketch on tracing paper laid over a photograph is a quick way of showing clients how their garden can be transformed.*

# CHAPTER SIX

# Developing the design

Now that the site plan, inventory and analysis have been completed, you are ready to begin working up the design. This is a daunting stage, and being confronted with a completely blank, pristine sheet of tracing paper, which should soon contain a new garden plan, can induce panic in the most seasoned designer. Often an uninspiring or difficult site can render the designer devoid of inspiration. One way out of this is to create a grid, using existing site lines, and then to experiment with abstract patterns and shapes which frequently reveal an entirely new concept. These shapes can then be linked to the existing site using the grid. This should ensure that the eventual design proportions are pleasing and well balanced.

## THE BUBBLE DIAGRAM

Long before you start to think of the style of garden you intend to create or of decorative details or planting designs, you must decide where you are going to place all the elements you intend to include in the garden and how these are going to function. At this point you will find it useful to have your clients' checklist and site analysis close to hand. Your clients may, for example, want a herb garden, in which case you must decide where in the garden would be the best place for this. If your clients intend to use the herbs for cooking you may at first think of placing the herb garden near to the kitchen. However, when you look at the orientation of the site, you may find that this part of the garden is very shaded and is, therefore, unsuitable for growing the many culinary herbs that require the sun. So you have to look at an alternative position. When you have found a suitable location for the herb garden, you must decide what is going to go next to it. Perhaps it would be pleasant to have the barbecue terrace here or the ornamental pool – or would this be the ideal place for the potting shed?

To help you decide what to put where, use a bubble diagram, drawn freehand on a sheet of tracing paper and laid over your site plan.

*This bubble diagram indicates roughly the proposed position of all required elements, the amount of space they will occupy, and how they will relate to domestic use.*

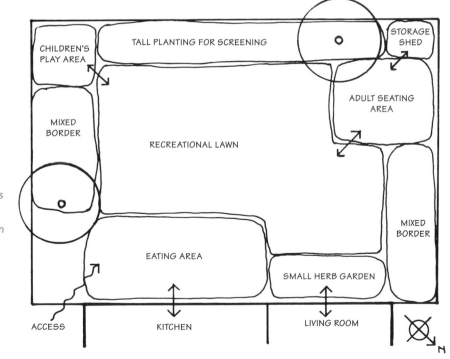

CHILDREN'S PLAY AREA

TALL PLANTING FOR SCREENING

STORAGE SHED

ADULT SEATING AREA

MIXED BORDER

RECREATIONAL LAWN

MIXED BORDER

EATING AREA

SMALL HERB GARDEN

ACCESS

KITCHEN

LIVING ROOM

N

Draw different sized bubbles, corresponding to all the elements and the space that you need to include in your design, making sure that you do not leave any gaps between the bubbles that you cannot identify.

These simple, functional drawings represent an exploratory stage of the design process and, being quick to complete, should enable you to look at many alternative sites for all the different elements in your new design.

## THE GRID SYSTEM

Once you know roughly what is going where and how much space you will need to allocate to the constituent elements of the garden, you are ready to start designing or to start converting your rough bubbles into specific shapes with defined edges. To help you get the proportions right, you may find it helpful to use a grid which should evolve from your site plan. The grid lines that you draw should spring from dominant lines in the site, such as the outside walls and corners of the house, protruding bays or extensions or wall buttresses. Using these existing structures to influence where new elements should go will help to coordinate old and new features.

In deciding how to divide up the site, look at the dimensions between the dominant site lines to see if they fall into some sort of module. You may, for instance, find that the distance from the corner of the house to the extension is 2 metres (2 yards), the distance from the extension to the next corner is 4 metres (4 yards) and the protrusion of the extension is 2 metres (2 yards). In this case a 2-metre (2-yard) grid would be ideal. For a larger house you may choose larger grid squares, following the rule that the scale of the grid should derive from the mass of the

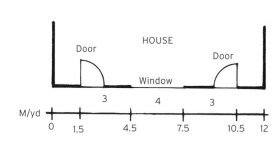

*The dominant features of the house suggest a 3-m (yd) grid.*

*The grid should be drawn up on tracing paper laid over the site plan.*

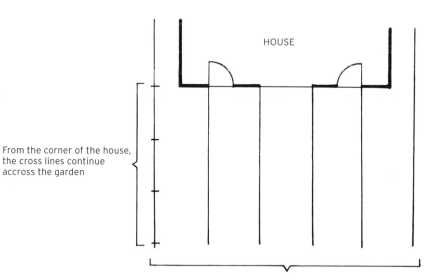

From the corner of the house, the cross lines continue accross the garden

These grid lines spring from the dominant house features, such as the door, walls and windows property. Many formal houses were built to a strict module of, say, 3 or 5 metres (3–5 yards), but in many cases new doors, windows or extensions have been added with no reference to the original module. In these instances you will need to experiment with your scale until you find a suitable way of dividing up the space. In some cases the module may not spring from the house itself but from some other features within the site, such as paths or gates. If the site is virgin land – perhaps simply a field surrounded by a fence – you can measure the entire length, say 30 metres (30 yards), and width, say 18 metres (18 yards), and simply divide it into equal sections, which in this case would give you a choice of a 6-, 3- or 2-metre (6-, 3- or 2-yard) grid.

If the site is large, you may wish to have a smaller grid, say 3 metres (3 yards) around the house, which can be doubled or trebled where the garden moves out into more open landscape. A square grid is much easier to use than a rectangular one, particularly if you are developing a circular theme for the design. Avoid the temptation of using graph paper squares as a basis for your grid – these are unlikely to correspond to dimensions that spring from the site itself, which is the main objective of this system. By basing your design framework on a grid, each area will be related to others in size, shape and proportion, giving cohesion and unity to your design.

Draw up your grid on tracing paper laid over your site plan. Once you have decided on the scale of your grid, use your parallel motion and set-square to draw in all the lines, both vertical and horizontal, to cover the whole area of the site.

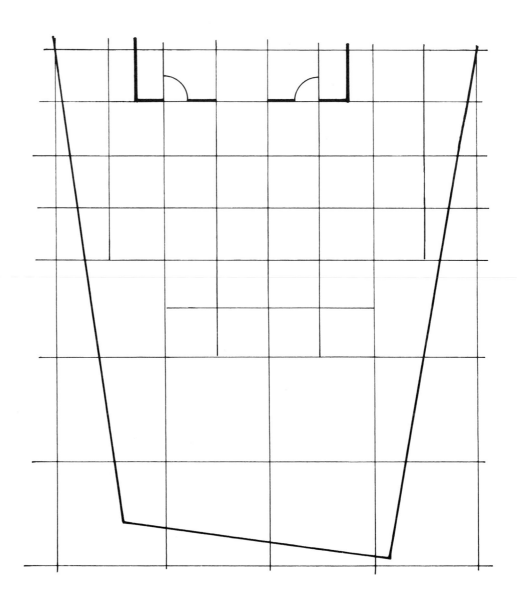

*The 3-m (yd) grid becomes a 6-m (yd) grid as it bleeds out into the landscape, encouraging larger, more natural shapes further from the house.*

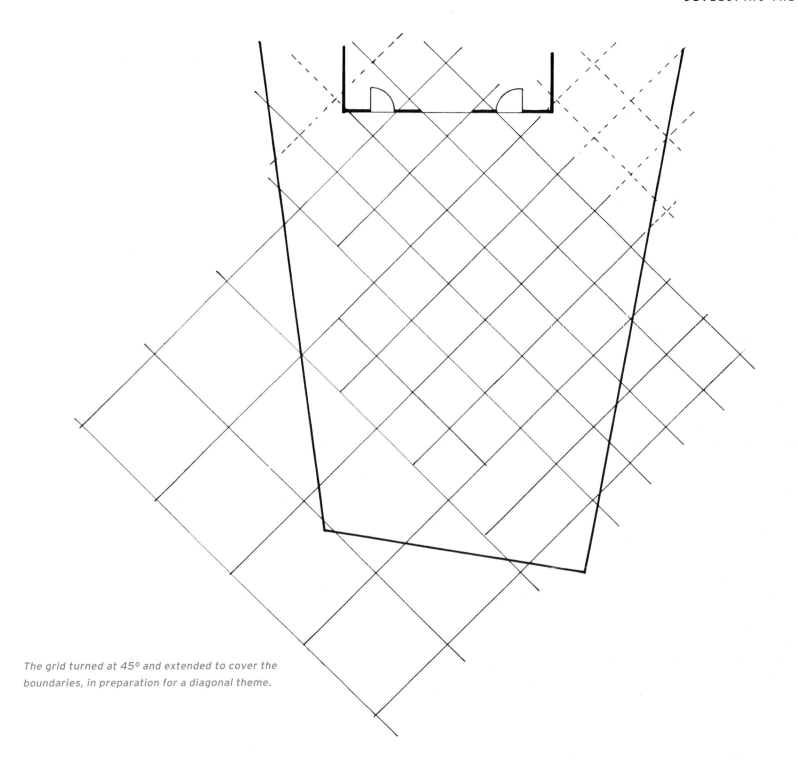

*The grid turned at 45º and extended to cover the boundaries, in preparation for a diagonal theme.*

## CREATING PATTERNS

With the grid in place you are now ready to try out different design themes based on geometric forms, such as circles and squares. If you are an inexperienced designer you should, at this point, temporarily abandon your bubble diagram and with it any preconceived ideas of how the garden should be laid out. What you are going to do now is to experiment with shapes of different sizes to produce several pieces of abstract art that you find visually and aesthetically pleasing.

Lay a fresh sheet of tracing paper over your site plan and grid and draw in different shapes or parts of shapes (straight lines, diagonals and curves), using the grid lines to help you position your shapes within your site and to determine their sizes – which should cover more, but not less, than one grid square.

If you find it difficult to know where to start, try using cut-out shapes, which again should be multiples of your grid squares and which you can first arrange then draw around. Different shapes can combine effectively provided they have a strong relationship, one shape springing from the dominant line in another. The way in which you combine these forms will be the basis of the garden's character, and the more you practise using and combining shapes, the more you will appreciate how different shapes have qualities that you can use to give a garden a feeling of order, informality or boldness. You will find that some of your patterns are static and restful, while others are more exciting and have a sense of movement.

*By tracing over a few selected lines, these interlocking shapes can be the basis for numerous other designs.*

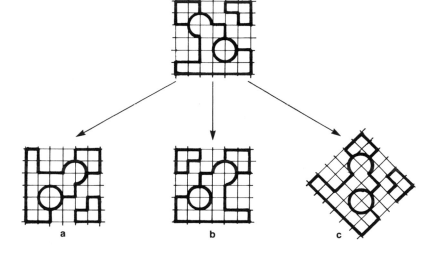

*In the search for an interesting design solution a pattern can be (a) rotated (b) reversed (c) turned at 45º.*

**a**    **b**    **c**

*Experiment with alternative combinations of mass and void.*

When you have created several patterns, experiment with them. Try rotating and reversing your patterns, or shading certain areas to divide your garden into positive and negative space, or areas of mass and void. All gardens are a combination of mass and void, but it is the proportion of the one to the other that is significant. One-third mass to two-thirds void is often an effective ratio.

Experimenting with shapes should help you to create totally fresh and new ideas to redesign a site, rather than simply tinkering with what is already there and readjusting it. Inspired with different ways of using the space, you are now ready to turn back to your bubble diagram and see how you can adapt your patterns to accommodate all the different elements required.

### Introvert and extrovert gardens

Garden designs tend to fall into two categories – the introvert garden, in which the interest is concentrated within the garden, by blurring the boundaries with planting, and the extrovert garden, in which the eye is encouraged to move beyond the garden boundaries to focus on attractive distant features, such as buildings or trees. On occasion, particularly in towns, one side of a garden may be overlooked by neighbouring houses, while the other side enjoys an open, sunny view. In this case, the attention may be concentrated on that open view, with the less attractive aspect being

View of neighbour's amenity area – compost heap and washing line

Develop introvert design for this area

View of high-rise building

Open sunny view

Develop extrovert design for this area

HOUSE

*This simple site analysis indicates good and bad views. Some views need to be hidden and others emphasized.*

*In this design strategically placed planting hides or distracts from bad views, while attention is drawn to good views.*

Screen planting

Terrace

HOUSE

treated as in an introvert garden, possibly disguised by a trellis or a thick band of planting.

## STATIC AND DYNAMIC DESIGNS

The choice of a particular design theme will depend on which is most appropriate for the site. The architectural style of the house may dictate whether the garden is to be formal or informal. Circular or strong, geometrical patterns may work well for small gardens, which usually require an introvert design. Small gardens are usually seen from the house as one complete picture, which must look good

throughout the year, with everything from hard landscaping through to planting, pots and garden furniture earning its keep. The design may be static or have a sense of movement.

*Right: This informal, dynamic design has a sense of movement.*

*Left: The simple shapes in this plan for a formal, static garden could be interpreted in numerous ways, depending on the material (water, paving, statuary, etc.) that is chosen for each space.*

HOUSE

## Diagonal themes

Long, thin gardens can often benefit from using a diagonal design, which draws the eye from one side of the garden to the other, helping to create an illusion of width. Frequently the garden can be divided into three equal spaces, with the diagonal layout aiding movement from one space to another. A similar sense of movement can be induced by using bold curves, with carefully placed trees acting as pivots to balance and alter the directional flow.

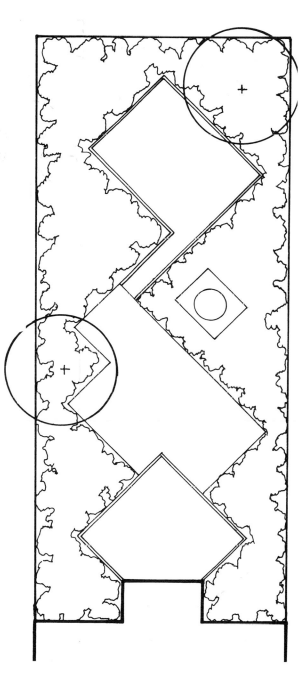

*Right: A diagonal design theme – which makes use of the longest stretch of the garden – creates an illusion of width.*

## TRANSLATING YOUR PATTERN INTO A PRELIMINARY DESIGN

### Horizontal and vertical planes

Although you are creating a flat plan, you must try to think of your garden as a three-dimensional object. Unless some interesting features or trees are to be retained the garden will appear very flat. You may wish to break it up by creating a change in level by using paths and steps to move from one space to another. Or you could include some raised beds with retaining walls, or pergolas, arches, pots and so on. Then, there are the plants and most importantly the trees. When they are carefully sited, trees can hold the horizontal plane together, balancing the flat spaces and acting as a pivot to turn corners or change direction or simply to lead the eye and encourage a sense of movement through the garden. Think also about the rest of your planting – not about the types of plants you intend to use but about their general height. You should label these areas as high, medium and low planting.

### Relating your plan to the human scale

Once you are happy with your design concept, you must start to refine your drawing, looking carefully at each element or space to make sure that the dimensions allowed for them will work practically and are properly related to the human scale. Ask yourself such questions as: Have I left enough space for a comfortable arrangement of chairs on the terrace? Are the paths wide enough? Have I allowed sufficient room for a car to turn on the drive?

You may well have to adjust the dimensions slightly, abandoning your grid

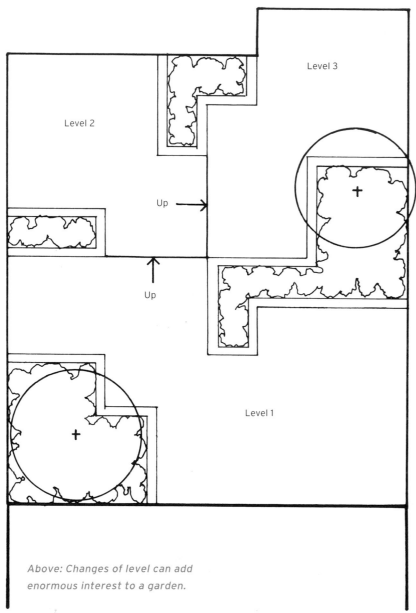

Level 3

Level 2

Up →

Up ↑

Level 1

*Above: Changes of level can add enormous interest to a garden.*

*Right: The bold curves of this design are accentuated by the circular shapes of the tree canopies.*

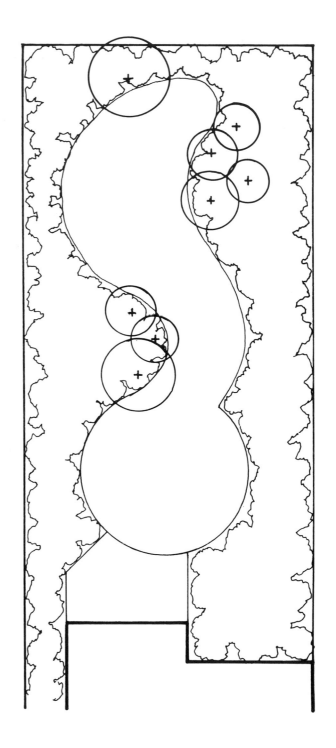

which, by this stage, will have served its purpose and can be put away.

You will now have some idea of how you wish the finished garden to look, but you may not know how to show this on a plan, perhaps being unsure of how much space to allow for structures such as paving, paths and pergolas. There is really no standard rule, the main factor being to allow enough space for the adult body, whether singly or en masse.

A simple way of relating the scale of a plan to the human frame is to draw a 'pin' man to scale beside the drawing. This can then be quickly measured to see how many times it will relate to the terrace or lawn. Think also about the machinery that may be required to build and maintain the garden. Similarly, if the only access is through a narrow alley, large artefacts or mature trees may prove a problem unless they are carried through the house. Too often, designers repeat interior dimensions in the garden, the effect being mean and cramped, as the landscape is seen on a much larger scale.

When you are representing hard and soft materials on a plan, the scale at which your plan is drawn will affect how much detail you are able to show. If a plan is drawn to a scale of 1 : 200 or 1 : 100, it will be necessary to rely on written information rather than a graphic representation, and the actual drawn details of the construction will be provided separately. It is unwise to show anything on a plan that is not drawn to scale – paving stones, for example – as it is likely that your builder may simply scale off from your plan. If the paving stones have been drawn to a larger size, he could order extremely large slabs that would be out of proportion with the rest of the garden.

The following points should be considered when you are planning the space:

**Terraces of paved areas** These are often adjacent to the house and link house and garden. The materials and construction are expensive, and to save money terraces are often smaller than is aesthetically pleasing. A terrace should derive its proportions from the bulk of the house. By taking the height of the eaves and measuring this out on the ground, a successful balance can be achieved. Some allowance for planting may be required adjacent to the house, and the terrace may, therefore, need to be projected out further.

**Paths** Often an edging, similar to the border of a carpet runner, is necessary to finish off a path visually. If necessary, additional space should be allowed for plants to flop over the edges, and in this case 1.5m (5ft) is necessary and will permit two people to walk almost abreast. Subsidiary paths can go down to 0.9m (3ft), but this will mean that people would have to progress in single file.

Ample room for parking and turning is necessary for drives and forecourts, the normal width for a drive being 3.5m (12ft), although this rather depends on whether the car is a Rolls Royce or a family saloon and how many visitors with similar cars will also wish to pass or park on the driveway.

**Steps** in the garden should have shallower risers and wider treads than an interior staircase. This will make the going easier. Steps should also be as wide as possible, with tread overhanging the riser to give a cast shadow or delineation, for both appearance's sake and for safety. Steps can also act as pivots or to change the direction of paths.

If, when you visit gardens, you carry a tape measure to measure steps, you will be able to note down what feels and looks comfortable.

**Water** When you include artificial ponds or areas of water you must also make provision for water to circulate, the size of the pump being in proportion to the amount of water involved. Perhaps a fountain or lake complete with island and landing stage is envisaged. Dealing with water can be a problem, so do not hesitate to call in expert advice for large or complex projects.

**Pergolas** must always lead somewhere, the main criteria being that adults can walk comfortably under them, which means that the verticals must be at least 2.5m (8f) high. If they are placed close together, they will appear even higher. An average spacing is about 3m (9ft) but much will depend on the material used. Sturdy brick or stone columns, perhaps supporting timber beams or railway sleepers, can be spaced further apart than more flimsy metal arches. Space should also be made for the plants, both at the base and up and across the verticals.

**Ground shaping or slopes** Ground shaping or creating contours and levels must also be considered before the main work begins. You survey may include spot levels, which indicate the height at the point (spot) at which they are taken. If they do not, you may need to ask advice. Earth-moving machinery may need to be employed. Isolated contours or mounds can look self-conscious and suspicious, as if they are trying to conceal something that the builder has left behind. It is far better to run proposed contours back into existing ones and to remove the excavated soil from the site.

# CHAPTER SEVEN

# Presentation of plans

The purpose of a plan, be it garden layout or planting, is to communicate your ideas to you client and ultimately to the contractor. If the client is being charged professional rates, he or she will expect a confident, professional drawing to which the garden can be constructed or planted.

At this stage your garden layout plan is a rough pencil drawing, probably on inferior quality tracing paper. When you present it to your client you will have refined it and retraced it onto the final sheet, which, apart from containing the plan, will be supplemented with vital writted information and enhanced with graphics. This final sheet will be copied and coloured up before it is presented to your client.

## SETTING OUT YOUR SHEET

When you are starting out as a garden designer you will need to design this final sheet, first for one paper size and then adapt it to fit other commonly used sizes – A1 ($33\frac{1}{8}$ x $23\frac{1}{2}$in) and A2 ($23\frac{1}{2}$ x $16\frac{1}{2}$in) are the most useful.

Each final sheet, which should be drawn on superior quality, 120gsm tracing paper, will need to contain the following:
• a title block
• an information panel
• a border
• a north point
These four items will remain constant, with the variable information, such as the client's name and the garden layout plan to be filled in later.

## TITLE BLOCK

The basic information to be included in a title block is:
• your name or company title, address, telephone and fax number, and email address
• your client's name or address
• drawing title (layout plan, planting plan, etc.)
• drawing number
• the scale or scales
• revisions
• date
• drawn by (initials only)
• statement of copyright
• disclaimer

The title block can be ornate or simple, depending on your own style. You may choose to include a logo to identify you work, to hint

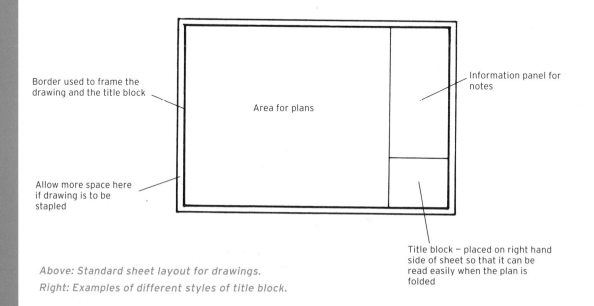

Border used to frame the drawing and the title block

Area for plans

Information panel for notes

Allow more space here if drawing is to be stapled

Title block – placed on right hand side of sheet so that it can be read easily when the plan is folded

*Above: Standard sheet layout for drawings.*

*Right: Examples of different styles of title block.*

at a particular style or to be witty or amusing, but usually simple, clear title blocks are the most effective.

The title block should always be placed in the lower right-hand corner of the information panel and should be approximately one-sixth to one-quarter of the overall height of that panel. The location is important because when the drawing is printed, it will be folded, and the title block must always appear uppermost. Choosing the style and size of the lettering or type face and selecting different sizes and spacing is a personal matter (see also page 17). Your choice will depend partly on your clientele and on how impressive you wish to appear.

Most designers now use word processors or computers to develop their title blocks and it is easy to alter the size and style of your lettering depending on the importance of the information. Computer-generated title blocks can then be transferred to the appropriate drawings, with any changeable information such as layout, planting plan or visuals and perhaps scale being adjusted for each drawing. Other designers prefer a more personal style and still devise their title blocks with stencils and freehand writing, either rewriting these afresh for each new plan or having them printed in batches on clear adhesive paper to be stuck on to the reverse side of the tracing paper drawing, variable information areas being left blank to be filled in later.

## Logos
Logos can help identify your practice and if you are having brochures and business cards

printed it is worth considering your company or corporate image, developing an image that can be used on all you literature and drawings – even your car or van.

### Scale

A statement of the scale or scales used on the drawing should appear within the title block, shown simply as 1 : 50, 1 : 100 and so on. If there are several drawing of different scales on a sheet, the words 'as shown' may be written

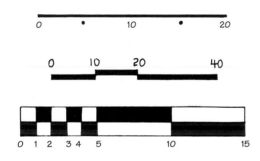

*Clients often find graphic scales easier to interpret than numerical scales.*

instead of the actual scale employed. The scale will then be shown clearly under each individual drawing. If the drawing is later reduced or enlarged, the statement of scale will no longer be accurate, and may then need to be altered or omitted. However, if a graphic scale is employed, this will remain accurate as it is inproportion to the plan and will reduce or enlarge accordingly.

### Copyright

A further note regarding the copyright of the drawing can be shown as © Rosemary

Alexander 2005. This clearly states that the copyright is the property of the designer and that the layout plan may not be copied without the express permission of the designer. Including this note can be a great help if clients ever mistakenly believe that they own the drawing.

### Disclaimers

Including the disclaimer 'This drawing may not be scaled. All dimensions to be checked on site' is standard practice on many drawings. The term dates from times when plans were drawn on linen, which was prone to stretch and distort the plan. Nowadays, it simply means that although the layout plan has been carefully been drawn to scale, the contractor is advised to check all dimensions on site before tendering or beginning construction, and it is used as a way of avoiding the responsibility for taking or transposing incorrect dimensions. This note should be set immediately above the title block.

### INFORMATION PANEL

The width of the information panel should be in proportion to the sheet used and to the information to be included – say 100mm (4in) for an A2 (23½ x 16½in) sheet, and perhaps 125mm or 150mm (5-6in) for an A1 (33⅛ x 23½in) sheet. Notes on hard landscaping or plant lists will soon fill this space. The title block should sit in the bottom right-hand corner of the information panel and should be large enough to be readable if the drawing is later reduced in size.

### BORDER

Borders are not essential, but having one will often enhance the look of a sheet. Once you have decided what type of border would be appropriate and where it should be located – 10mm (about ½in) from the edge of the sheet is usual – you can start to draw in the border in ink, using thick or thin lines. The right-hand side of the border can then become the outside line of the information panel.

### THE PLAN AND HOW TO PLACE IT

The placing of the plan on the sheet determines how the finished garden layout plan will look. The entire sheet should be thought of as a piece of graphic design and be set out accordingly. Having designed the sheet layout, you must decide how best to arrange all the information that should be included.

First there will be the plan itself. At this stage it may be best to turn the sheet containing the site or base plan around to see how best it can be located on this fresh sheet, and to sketch out a dummy layout before beginning any drawing. The plan will need to be titled, and some of these titles may be extensive. Make sure that the sheet is large enough to accommodate all necessary information, because it will not be effective if data are squashed up or cramped.

Second, other items may need to be included – a section through the site, a detail of steps or an enticing bird's eye perspective, for example. Often these are drawn up separately, but this depends on the size of the sheet, the size of the garden, the scale at which it is drawn and how much back-up information you wish to show. The size of these additional drawings should be carefully considered or, better still, completed in pencil and set up, rather like a collage, under your chosen sheet to see how much space they will take up before any final work is done.

If there is any danger of overcrowding, either use a larger sheet or reduce the scale of the layout plan or put some information on a second sheet. The usual technique is to situate the main plan towards the bottom of the sheet, either in the centre or slightly to the left, and to arrange the other information around it. All lines should begin at the same invisible margin, and here the graph paper backing sheet is an excellent guide. Care and time taken in thinking through or pasting up the sheet before actually inking in will save time and recriminations later.

*Below: When positioning a plan consider from which direction the clients view their garden.*

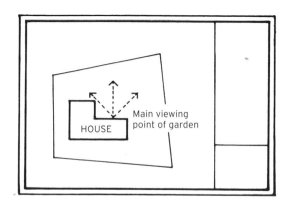

*Below: The dimensions of your drawing will determine where you put labels.*

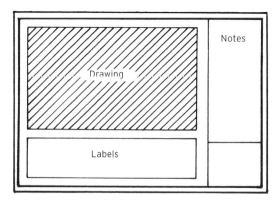

## North arrows

All garden layout or planting plans should include in the bottom right-hand corner adjacent to the title block an arrow or a north point indicating the northerly direction of the site. All that is required is an arrow and the letter N, but this can be shown in a variety of ways and be drawn with pen, stencils or computer graphics. Once a pleasing design has been worked out, it can be used for every drawing, with only the direction being adjusted, according to the site aspect. The north point, therefore, can be added to the tracing paper sheets only when the position of the plan has been decided.

Once everything to be shown has been allocated a position, drawing up the final layout plan can begin, and should proceed quickly without too many changes or erasures.

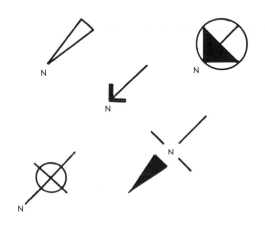

*Above: Different styles of north arrow. The 'N' is optional for most of those shown here.*

# CHAPTER EIGHT

# The garden layout plan

The garden layout plan is the drawing from which the new garden will normally be set out and constructed, but before this can be undertaken, the plan must, of course, be approved by your client, who will want to see how it fulfils the brief you have been given.

## DRAWING UP YOUR LAYOUT PLAN

The layout plan must be drawn accurately to scale so that everything shown on it can be reproduced in the garden. If your plan is drawn to a scale of 1 : 100 or even at 1 : 50 it may be too small to show in detail how you propose to construct such features as steps, walls or pergolas. These details can be shown on a separate drawing or detail sheet but if there is space around the plan, they may even be illustrated on the same sheet to help your client to interpret your ideas.

Before beginning to draw up your garden layout plan on your final sheet, it is useful to know the normal sequence that is followed.

When you have decided where to position your plan, trace this in ink or pencil onto your final sheet (complete with title block etc) from your rough layout plan. This plan should show all areas of hard landscaping as well as lawn and water on the site. Unless the site is very small, it will not usually include details of planting. NB do NOT ink in over your pencil lines as the ink will not 'take' – the graphite creates a barrier between the ink and the paper.

If, as is usual, you intend to create a separate planting plan, take a copy of your garden layout plan now, before you add in the labels, titling or any extra drawings, but with the title block and north point. This copy, showing the hard landscaping with empty planting areas, can later be developed into the planting plan.

After taking a copy of your unlabelled garden layout plan, you can add any extra back-up drawings you may wish to have on this sheet, such as details, elevations and sections.

Once the drawings are all in place, you are ready to label the original. Many clients will ask you to do a garden layout plan first before they decide whether they want to commission a planting plan from you. To persuade them to do this, you may like to hint at your planting intentions on your garden layout plan, using appealing, descriptive phrases such as 'scented border to include lilacs, roses and lilies' or 'winter garden to include hellebores, bulbs and early-flowering shrubs'.

### Pen nib sizes

Before you start to ink things in think about the nib sizes of the thicker nibs being used for the more dominant features. A variety of pen sizes gives enormous interest and relief to even the simplest drawing. Stencils or computer-generated labelling can be used to label certain areas, such as house, garage or lawn, or use your own handwriting – this saves your time and the client's money and gives a personal informal touch to a drawing.

Felt-tip ———————————

0.70 ———————————

0.50 ———————————

0.35 ———————————

0.25 ———————————

*A variation of nib size or thickness of line makes the drawing easier to understand.*

## PROCEDURE FOR DRAWING UP A FINAL PLAN

Before you pick up your drawing pens or pencils and heavier quality tracing paper, make sure that all the information on your preliminary drawings, now to be shown on your final plan, is firmly stuck down in your desired position on your graph paper backing sheet. Make sure in due course there will be sufficient space around the plan for labelling. Then stick down your heavier sheet of tracing paper. Now study your layout and what is to be drawn.

When you are satisfied with your layout, take a sheet of scrap paper and list the various elements to be drawn in sequence of importance, noting down what nib size you will use for each; the boundaries, house and tree canopies for example, should be drawn in your heaviest nib size whereas hard landscaping and planting should be drawn with a finer nib such as a 0.35 or 0.25. Do this in logical order until you have included everything that is to be drawn.

Remember that the time you spend will be reflected in your client's bill! You will want to execute your work well but as quickly and cleanly as possible. To avoid picking up and putting down the various nib sizes and making mistakes, begin by first drawing in everything running horizontally across your sheet with your largest nib size balanced against your parallel motion. Next use the same nib size to drawn in all your vertical elements, balancing your pen against your set square. Continue like this, moving down through your nib sizes until every element is drawn in. By working across from right to left if you are left-handed) you will avoid smudging the ink before it dries.

*Using shadow patterns on the shady side of plants makes a drawing more lifelike.*

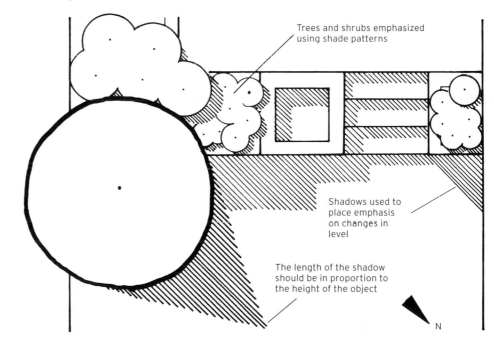

Trees and shrubs emphasized using shade patterns

Shadows used to place emphasis on changes in level

The length of the shadow should be in proportion to the height of the object

## ENHANCING YOUR PLAN WITH SHADOW EFFECTS

As well as varying nib sizes to add depth to your plan, you can also apply shade and shadow effects, either to the original or to a copy for your client. Unless the shadows cast at various times of day are a crucial aspect of your design, you need not worry about knowing exactly where they will fall through-out the day and at different times of the year. Your aim is to enhance the graphic quality of the plan and to make it more realistic and therefore easier for the client to understand.

Although the shadow casting need not be accurate, you can assume for the purposes of this exercise that the shadow will fall to the north side of all the objects in your plan and that the length of the shadow will be equal to the height of the object. Because you are using shadow for emphasis, you should use it selectively and resist the temptation to add it to everything. You may feel that on your garden layout plan you would like to emphas-ize the hard landscaping only and then, later, on your planting plan, the planting only. The choice is yours.

One rather subtle way of adding shadow to your original is by shading the back of the drawing with a soft pencil. You can then smudge the pencil with your finger to produce an even, soft effect. This will reproduce well by the dyeline process (see page 127), although the technique is rather less successful when it is photocopied.

## INDICATING DIFFERENT STRUCTURES AND SURFACES

In drawing up the garden layout plan, it is usual first to locate the drawing centrally on the sheet, then to draw the house or any buildings in a heavy, continuous line, breaking it where doors and windows occur. In garden design, it is not usual to show the house wall as double thickness.

### Boundaries

Boundaries are also drawn in at this stage. If they are marked by a free-standing wall this is usually shown as a double line of equal thickness, but if the boundaries are unfenced they are shown as a broken line.

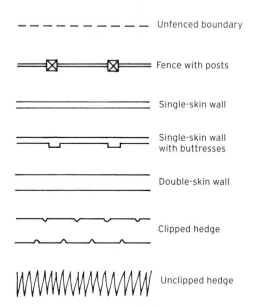

Unfenced boundary

Fence with posts

Single-skin wall

Single-skin wall with buttresses

Double-skin wall

Clipped hedge

Unclipped hedge

### Doors

The door is indicated by a single line at right angles to the wall, the swing of its opening edge being achieved by a semicircle. Occasionally, when the door lines at right angles may be confused with other lines on the drawing, they can be drawn at a lesser angle provided the same technique is used throug-out the drawing.

### Windows

The representation of windows differs according to whether they are of wood or metal, and they cannot be shown satisfactorily at less than 1 : 10. A single, finer line should be used.

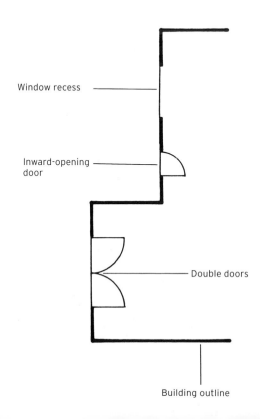

Window recess

Inward-opening door

Double doors

Building outline

Cobbles – laid in circular pattern

Gravel

Stone setts

Brick – herringbone

Brick – basketweave

Brick – stretcher bond

Uniform paving slabs

Random rectangular cut stone

### Terraces or paved areas

Where possible, the material used for a terrace or paved area should be in keeping with the house and the locality – a combination of stone and brick, perhaps, or stone with a brick surround. If the budget is tight, gravel may be a cheaper alternative. Depending on your scale, gravel can be indicated by tiny circles interspersed with dots or simply by dots.

### Paths

Paths can be of many different materials – stone, brick, concrete or gravel – but they should also be in keeping with the architecture. They can be illustrated to show the material and, in the case of brick or other

Brick path — Stone edge

Planted area — Timber edging — Grass — Hoggin

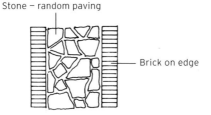

Stone – random paving — Brick on edge

paving, the directional flow. Any edgings such as brick or a timber strip to separate gravel and borders or grass must also be indicated. Remember that when they are seen from above, every object on the plan should be clearly defined and even in the case of narrow or thin edgings the thickness or both sides must be shown by two lines.

### Steps

Steps should be drawn to show the desired number of treads and the width of each. Arrows should always point upwards, with the central line of the arrow beginning at the outer edge of the first riser. Often the word 'up' will be included, and for clarity, risers may be

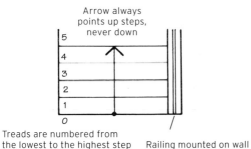

Arrow always points up steps, never down

Treads are numbered from the lowest to the highest step    Railing mounted on wall

numbered in order beginning with the lowest, the first riser being shown by a dot on the line of the arrow. If the steps are flanked by a railing or retaining wall, this must also be shown. The height of each riser, which cannot be shown on a flat plan, can be stated either by titling or as a note in the information panel.

### Ramps

Should have an arrow pointing in the 'up' direction and should be titled as 'ramp'.

The angle of rise – 15° maximum – should be shown on a section (see Chapter 9).

Record the gradient and the height at the top and bottom of a ramp

### Walls

Walls are differentiated by using a thicker nib size for the outer wall. Retaining and free-standing walls can be of various heights. A low retaining wall of four or five brick courses can double as an extra seating area, while higher, free-standing walls may need expansion joints and buttresses to support them.

The final course or coping of a wall has a crucial effect on its appearance, and it needs to be thought through carefully. Both coping and the bond must be shown in an elevation or detail, or labelled. If the corners of the wall are to be finished off in a particular way, this, too should be shown. The height of the wall can be written in or included in your notes. Fences are shown as a double line, while small rectangles indicate the upright fence posts.

Concrete block wall with concrete-capped piers

Brick retaining wall with mitred corner

Dry stone wall

### Ponds and areas of water

To indicate a still stretch of water, draw broken lines to simulate light shining on water. A fountain can be shown as a small circle with other circles representing ripples emanating from it. In both cases, titling will help to clarify the meaning.

Still water

Water with fountain

### Pergolas and other ornamental features

Where vertical and horizontal dimensions of ornamental features meet, both should be shown, and because the drawing is to scale, the size at which they are drawn will depend on the material used – stone, brick, timber or metal. Arches are indicated in the same way as pergolas. If plants are being drawn to cover them, they can also be shown, provided they do not confuse the drawing.

Pergola with square posts

Arch with circular posts

### Statues, urns and pots

Statues or urns usually have to stand on plinths, which should be in proportion with whatever stands on them. They are usually shown as circles on a square base, or simply as a circle within a thicker circle, both drawn with

Statue or urn on plinth

A group of circular pots

a circle template, to indicate the inner and outer thickness of the object. Planting within may be shown if wished.

## Ground shaping or slopes

Contours are shown as a broken line, within existing contours having longer dashes than proposed contours. Their height, which should be related to a datum height or level, can be written beside the lines. The closer the contours, the steeper the gradient. Slopes or embankments can be shown as Vs or as arrows pointing downwards, and their proximity will again indicate the gradient.

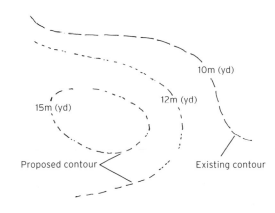

10m (yd)

12m (yd)

15m (yd)

Proposed contour

Existing contour

Embankment for curving slope

Lowest side

Embankment

Gradient between upper and lower terrace

## Drainage, irrigation and electricity

Drainage, irrigation and electricity must also be incorporated at the design stage, because work may need to be carried out before the main construction begins and each arrangement will vary according to the site limitations. These hidden costs can soon mount up, and the must, therefore, be included in the written specification to the contractor that should accompany the design.

Sometimes it is necessary to indicate the junction of drains at the downpipes of the house, and this is done with a small circle and appropriate letters. Gullies are shown as a square, and a crossfall to them is indicated with a small arrow. Manhole covers are shown as a bisected rectangle and the letters MH.

Irrigation is simply shown as a broken line, and the position of any sprinklers in a lawn, for instance, can be marked with a small cross and titled.

Electricity cables are also indicated with a broken line.

Irrigation and electric cables and lighting points should be titled to avoid confusion. Wall sockets are normally indicated as a half circle.

Drainage

Pipe    House wall

S.P.    Soil pipe

S.+ V.P.    Soil and vent pipe

W.P.    Waste pipe

R.W.P.    Rain water pipe

G    Gulley

Crossfall

M.H.    Manhole cover

Electricity and irrigation

Pop-up sprinkler    Irrigation cable

Electricity cable also shown as a dashed line

Wall socket

### Alterations or additions

A clear distinction must be made between what exists and what is proposed, with only the minimum essential outlines of the former being drawn, the new work being indicated in the usual manner. Proposed walls are usually shown as outlines in a heavier black line, and existing walls are drawn in a finer line or in pencil.

Communication is the main objective in presenting a garden layout plan to a client, and the plan should, therefore, look as realistic as possible. There are really no set rules for symbols of garden structures, but whatever is shown must be drawn to scale. It can be difficult and time consuming to draw a realistic brick path to a scale of 1:100 or even at 1:50, and the average client would probably prefer a smaller bill than to see every brick carefully illustrated.

In order to explain what is envisaged, a small, more detailed sketch, at a scale of 1:5, 1:10 or 1:20, can accompany the layout plan to give a clear idea of the intentions. The symbols should be drawn in different thicknesses of line depending on the dominance of the feature – house and tree will be indicated in a heavier line than pots, brick edging or ground-cover planting, for example. Many designers spend too much time on elaborate graphics. Clear, simple plans are less time consuming to produce and, therefore, less expensive for the client.

## LABELLING OR TITLING

One of the most confusing elements of drawing up a plan, labelling can make or break a drawing. Your labelling must be neat, legible, especially if your drawing is to be reduced at any stage) and to avoid moving the sheet or bending, should all run in the same direction across the sheet. Varying your ink nib or pencil thicknesses according to the importance of the different elements should follow the same procedure as in drawing lines. It is up to you whether you prefer to use computer-generated lettering, stencils or handwriting – the former two are advisable if more than one person is working on a drawing.

Some designers label each item directly on to that item while others prefer to extend labelling lines beyond the plan; either is acceptable as long as it is easy to follow and read.

Labelling on either side or above and below the plan should either all begin from the same invisible outside line, or if there are many items, every alternate item should be indented.

Various aids may speed up this process. Lined sheets of foolscap of varying distances can be accumulated, for example, and used under your tracing paper as guides.

### Information panels

The beginning of your information panel should sum up in two or three concise sentences exactly what you are trying to achieve with your garden layout plan. This should hark back to the client's brief and serve as a reminder of what you were asked to do. Because much of the information you may wish to give both your client and the contractor is too extensive to write on the plan. This should now be included in the information panel. Although you may have stated heights, widths, and materials in your labelling these details now need to be taken further to form a 'mini specification', which will help your client understand your intentions and allow the contractor to price for the work. A typical example might be 'Low brick retaining wall height 0.500mm (1ft 8in)' stated on the plan, but in the information panel this would be expanded on to state 'Low retaining wall – bricks to be of Ibstock 'Brindle' laid Single Flemish bond, coping to be of Marshalls 'Rustic', or reconstituted stone', or a similar phrase to indicate that you have thought through what material is to be used and how the wall should be built. Both your garden layout plan and your planting plan should include this information panel in the column above the title block at the right-hand side of your plan. Remember to also include a North point and perhaps a graphic scale.

Steps into folly garden. Tread 40cm riser to be confirmed on site. Brick lights to be inserted either side of the steps

Clipped evergreen hedges no more than 40cm high

Slate seating providing contrast to colour of walling and offering a reverse view of the garden

HOUSE

Raised blockwork border 45cm high

Standard ivy trained into gothic shape. Height to be determined by arc of water feature

Paving: Marshall's Saxon paving (natural) with 600 x 600 x 35 slabs edged with Drivesett tegula blocks 240 x 160 x 50 in slate colour

Fig and other planting to be removed as agreed on site

Light to fall from new windows onto terrace (the effect will be subtle)

Clipped evergreen standards up to 160cm gently underlit

Raised bed with soft planting

Existing acacia to remain

Silver bowls (2) with submerged pump and reservoir. Water to be pumped from one bowl to other through ivy and pumped below ground to first bowl

*It is vital that annotations are clear and that any labelling lines are easy to follow. In this layout plan, care has been taken to clearly show the different hard and soft landscape materials used in the design.*

# CHAPTER NINE

# Sections, elevations and construction details

Although the garden layout plan has been completed, many clients cannot understand or visualize a flat plan, and some additional explanatory drawings may be necessary. The contractor or garden builder may also require further drawings to clarify the overall concept and, although spot heights and levels should have been included on the layout plan, a section or sections taken through the garden will make the various heights and levels understood.

Section-elevation

Plan view

*Drawing a section-elevation shows the three-dimensional effect of a plan.*

To be useful to both client and contractor, a section or elevation should explain something that cannot be understood from the flat garden layout plan. First decide what you need to show, then study your layout plan from all angles until you have decided which angle or view will show most. Do you want to show only what happens above ground, or would it be more useful to also show what goes on below the soil level – perhaps a sunken pool or 'cut and fill' proposals. You will need to title your drawing appropriately so it is necessary to understand the difference between the different types of drawings. Remember always to indicate on your layout plan exactly where the cut line of the drawing begins, ends, and from which angle it is seen.

Sections, elevations and section-elevations are all used to show the detail of vertical elements in the garden, whether it is the whole garden that needs to be shown or only details of a specific item, such as a pond, for construction purposes.

## Sections
In a true section, no surface details are shown, only the outlined shapes of elements along the cut line are included; these may be useful for showing changes of level and for some construction drawings.

## Elevations
Elevations, on the other hand, do show surface details, as well as elements beyond and, sometimes, just before the cut line itself is not shown. Architects often use elevations to show details of house facades, and they can be useful for showing planting areas.

Section

Elevation

Section-elevation

## Section-elevations

As their name suggests, these are a combination of sections and elevations. They are often referred to as landscape sections or simply sections, although they are not true sections, showing both a prominent cut line and surface details of vertical features on and beyond the cut line. Section-elevations are quick and easy to draw because all the vertical objects shown are drawn at their proper scale, no matter how far they are from the cut line.

Normally, two sections are sufficient for the small or average sized garden, but if there are several changes of level or if the garden is large, more may be necessary. Usually, the first section is taken through the entire length of the garden and the second section is taken across the width of the garden. In each case the exact beginning and end should be clearly indicated on both the plan and the sectional drawing. For example, the first section may be extended from the house wall to the distant boundary and may include only the terrace, lawn and some planting, while the second section may run from the boundary wall to the opposite boundary wall, but will include a greenhouse, steps, arch, tree or anything else that occurs on the section line shown. There is no standard point at which a section should be taken, but it is sensible to carry the line through at a point where there are various changes in level, both above and below ground level, or where there is a certain amount of vertical interest to be explained.

## Enlarging the scale

If the plan is drawn to a scale of 1 : 100 or smaller, it may be difficult to show in sufficient detail what is going on unless the proposed garden is on a steep slope that is being transformed into a series of terraces. If necessary, the section can be drawn in a larger scale, say to 1 : 50 or even 1 : 20. Occasionally, the horizontal scale may remain at 1 : 100, while the vertical scale is shown at 1 : 50, but this can be rather distorting and should be used only for showing reshaped landforms, but not for the average small garden.

It is as important to show what goes on below ground level as to show what happens above. This may be a swimming pool, pond, sunken terrace, structural foundations of walls, hedges, tree pits or existing tree roots.

If, at each side of the section, the overall height is also indicated to scale, there can be no misunderstanding. It also helps to relate the proposals to surrounding buildings. Sometimes it is useful to include with the section a drawn-to-scale human figure, perhaps standing under the pergola, so that the client may identify with the scale.

## Groundworks or contouring

Sections are also necessary where major groundworks occur or where there is recontouring or 'cut and fill'. The existing land formation level can be shown in one way and the proposed levels in another, with key spot heights always being indicated as on the layout plan. This may help the client to understand the proposal and to assist in calculations for moving or importing soil on the site. It is

*Right: This section shows the 'cut and fill' method of creating terracing from a slope. The soil removed is used as fill for the lower part of the site.*

possible that you have overlooked the need for access for earth-moving equipment or the removal and reconstruction of a gateway or part of a wall to allow vehicular access will be an additional and perhaps unforeseen expense.

**Where to place sections on a sheet**

These sections can either be drawn on a separate sheet or, if there is space, they can be included on the same sheet as the layout plan. Place the section in an easily identifiable position so that its relationship to the layout plan is obvious. This may mean having one section running horizontally across the sheet and the other running vertically, or both sections running horizontally. Choose whatever is clear and looks effective, while at the same time making sure that any figures or writing can be easily read without the reader having to twist his or her head sideways. Because it is larger, the layout plan is usually best placed lower on the sheet, with a section or sections shown above it, and the name and location of the section indicated on the plan, with arrows indicating the direction from which they have been drawn, such as A-B or A-A, B-B.

## DETAILED DRAWINGS

Depending on the subject being shown and the complexity of the detail to be shown, these drawings can be at a scale of 1 : 50 down to 1 : 20, 1 : 10, or even at 1 : 1. As they may be interpreted as actual construction drawings, it is unwise to include such detailed drawings unless you are completely familiar with or knowledgeable about how to build them. Unless you are a qualified architect, landscape

architect or surveyor, it may be wiser to show the contractor a rough sketch, photograph or a real-life example of what you intend, because the client could take legal action against you should the construction detail prove faulty.

*Examples of detail drawings, drawn to scale.*

## CONSTRUCTION DETAILS

It is frequently impossible to show on garden layout plans the detailed proposals for the construction of paths, paving, steps, arches or other hard landscaping items. In the construction of roof terraces, where there may be a heavy weight load for instance, it may be necessary to show each layer of material, hard and soft, to make the method of building absolutely clear. Certain areas might need to be drawn in greater detail, showing the internal structure of all the components and how they fit together. These drawings are again largely sectional, and they should be drawn to scale, indicating the materials used, and their dimension and thickness shown with strong pen or pencil lines, the written dimensions also being included to avoid misinterpretation.

Construction details are not usually drawn on the same sheet as the garden plan but on a separate sheet or sheets of tracing paper, which are then given to the builder or engineer. Occasionally a designer may plan the garden layout, but may then seek the advice of or enlist the services of an architect, architectural technician or other professional to carry out the detailed construction drawing, particularly if these are to be classed as work drawings, from which the subject will be built.

If the main purposes of your detailed drawings is to help communicate ideas to your client, you may wish to position them around the garden layout plan. This may not be an approved standard practice and it can be confusing, but if there is space on the sheet, it may be aesthetically pleasing and help to sell the concept.

*Below: Simple construction sections, drawn to scale, can be filed and reused, with minor modifications, on many different projects.*

Elevation of entrance gate

HORIZONTAL BAR 20X20
VERTICAL BAR 12X12
VERTICAL BAR WITH FINIAL 20X20 AT 120 CENTRES
HORIZONTAL BAR 20X20
GROUND SUPPORT AT PANEL CENTRES. PANELS 1400 LONG, WELDED TOGETHER

Section of front wall at post

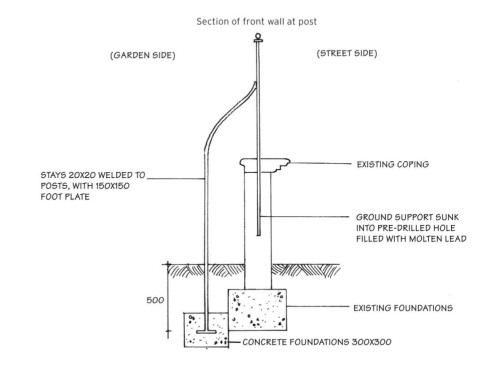

(GARDEN SIDE)    (STREET SIDE)

STAYS 20X20 WELDED TO POSTS, WITH 150X150 FOOT PLATE

EXISTING COPING

GROUND SUPPORT SUNK INTO PRE-DRILLED HOLE FILLED WITH MOLTEN LEAD

EXISTING FOUNDATIONS

CONCRETE FOUNDATIONS 300X300

Section of pool

Brick retaining wall
Fountainhead

Waterproof connection attaching
waterproof cable to output cable

50mm
overhang

Stone coping

To power supply

Single layer brick
facing

500mm
depth

Hose pipe

50mm concrete smoothed
over dried bottom layer

100mm concrete
base reinforced with
wire netting

Submersible
pump

Concrete sealant (for sealing and
for neutralizing lime in concrete)

BACK

Scale 1:10

FRONT

Section of concrete sett steps

30cm

20cm

Concrete setts in
mortar bed
All joints 10

10cm

Insitu concrete

Weldmesh

Hardcore

15cm

10cm

10cm

25cm

Section
(Scale 1:10)

25cm

Section of timber retaining wall

100    50

CAPPING NAILED TO
POSTS AND SIDING

50

100

HT
VARIES

POSTS AT EITHER SIDE
– DECKING SIDE AND
BOUNDARY WALL

SIDING CHAMFERED 10
ON FACING SIDE
NAILED TO POSTS WITH
GALVANISED NAILS

FINISHED GRADE

600

POSTS SET IN GROUND IN
PREPARED HOLE AND
BACKFILLED WITH
SUBSOIL AND RAMMED

CLAYWARE PIPE 100 IN
COURSE GRAVEL

*A continental approach has been adopted for this country garden. To make full use of the space, the garden has been divided into a series of rooms connected by walkways, with extensive timber decking around the house providing areas for sitting and for entertaining.*

N

Existing sycamore trees

Existing poplar tree

Dense evergreen screening and ground cover

Plinth for statue

Gravel path

Pavilion

Ground level wash lighting

Spring and autumn border

Spring and summer scented border

Existing pyracantha

C

Scent and foliage interest

Lawn

Foliage interest

Ground level wash lighting

New trees

Cloistered gravel walk

Sitting area

Aromatic foliage and scented flowers

Silhouette planting

Basement well

Existing holly tree re-positioned

Basement well

House

Basement well

UP

Gravel path

Fastigiate conifers

Dustbin cover

Section

Section

*In this garden layout plan the design has a strong ground pattern. Lush planting provides privacy and shelter and a pergola – clearly shown in the first section – screens the terrace from overlooking houses. Enticing descriptions of proposed planting will often encourage a client to commission a detailed planting plan.*

EAST FACING SECTION 'B'

*The brief for this site was to design an intimate, secluded, yet formal garden. The space has been divided to create a series of distinct, symmetrical areas linked by hedges.*

## STANDARD SYMBOLS

There may be no standard way of indicating materials on a layout plan, but in sections or elevations there are accepted standard methods, and these must be followed so that the different materials can be easily distinguished. There are conventional ways of indicating materials in general use, in which all lines or hatching are drawn diagonally at 45º, the spacing of the lines varying according to the scale of the drawing, but the general proportions being followed. Where large areas of cross-hatching need to be shown, it is only necessary to indicate a portion near the edge or ends, the hatching gradually being faded out towards the middle. If there is any possibility that the symbols used on any of your plans are likely to cause confusion, a legend or key may be drawn in the right-hand information panel.

### Abbreviations of words

There is an accepted conventional standard in the abbreviation of words commonly used on drawings, and using these also helps to avoid confusion. Although it is unlikely that all of these will be used in a garden design, familiarity with them may help you decipher other drawings.

### Materials and general terms

| | |
|---|---|
| Aggregate | Agg |
| Approved | appd |
| Approximate | approx |
| Asbestos | Asb |
| Asphalt | Asph |
| Bench mark | BM |
| Bitumen | Bitn |
| Brickwork | Bwk or B |

| | |
|---|---|
| British Standard | BS |
| Cast iron | CI |
| Cement | Cem |
| Centre line | CL or C |
| Centre to centre | c/c |
| Concrete | Conc |
| Diameter | dia |
| Drawing | Dwg |
| Galvanized | Galv |
| Ground level | GL |
| Gully | G |
| Height | ht |
| Insulated or insulation | insul |
| Invert | inv |
| Left hand | LH |
| Macadam | MAC |
| Manhole | MH |
| Not to scale | NTS |
| Number | No |
| Radius | rad |
| Rain-water pipe | RWP |
| Reinforced concrete | RC |
| Rain-water outlet | RWO |
| Round | rd |
| Sketch | sk |
| Soil and vent pipe | S&VP |
| Soil pipe | SP |
| Specification | Spec |
| Square | Sq |
| Standard Wire Gauge | SWG |
| Stand pipe | St P |
| Street gully | SG |
| Tongued and grooved | T&G |
| Traced | Tcd |
| Volume | vol |
| Waste pipe | WP |
| Waste and vent pipe | W&VP |
| Water closet | WC |

## INDICATING MATERIALS ON VERTICAL CONSTRUCTIONS

The following are the accepted ways of indicating materials in sections

### Brickwork
At scales of 1 : 100 and less, brickwork is indicated in section by two solid 45º diagonal lines drawn close together. It is easiest to draw in the diagonal lines by setting out the heights of the courses on a vertical line at the left-hand side of the sheet and then drawn them by using a 45º set-square balanced against your T-square or parallel motion.

### Stonework
Stone walls are indicated in section as solid black at 1 : 100 and smaller scales. When they are drawn at a larger scale – 1 : 50 or 1 : 20 – the individual stones can be shown.

### Timber
Continuous thin lines at the appropriate scale are used to represent vertical or horizontal timber in section at scales of 1 : 50 and less.

### Reinforced concrete
This can be shown in the conventional representation in various scales.

*Conventional methods of representing materials on sectional drawings.*

Brickwork (at 1:20)

Brickwork (at 1:50)

Brickwork (at 1:100)

Brickwork (at scales of over 1:100)

Cement

Soil — Note that soil is usually hatched freehand

Hardcore

Concrete — Show the aggregate in small areas

Timber

Masonry

# CHAPTER TEN

# The planting plan

All garden designers have their own particular method of working up a planting plan, and it is unlikely that any two designers would approach or carry through their planting design in the same way. The most important thing is to find a simple, and therefore relatively quick, method of showing the interplay between plants – not only for a client, but also for you, as the designer, to check that there is sufficient contrast or balance of form, texture and colour in the proposed planting.

## WHAT TO AIM FOR

Some designers who may have a very clear idea of the desired effect do a quick outline elevation before beginning their planting plan and find it easier to work from this, backwards, as it were, to the flat plan. Other designers, faced with an empty planting area, immediately begin thinking about what each plant will be and give the full botanical name to each circle or outline shape as they work up the plan. There are no hard and fast rules – simply experiment until you find a method that suits you.

Speed is important because you will charge your client for your time.

As with most designers, your particular graphic style will develop with practice. Experiment with different techniques, try to see the work of other designers and look at how they present their planting plans. Are their plans sufficiently straightforward for a 'non-visual' client to understand? Would they be easy to plant from?

Working up a planting plan is often the most testing part of a garden designer's work. The expertise lies in selecting, grouping together and using plants to achieve certain requirements, such as dramatic foliage in a narrow, dry border, or using pale shades to lighten a dark, shady area. Although the individual plants must be able to cope with the constraints of the site, it is the grouping or massed effect of the planting that will provide the visual interest.

Most clients are not interested in obscure plants. The usual requests are for year-round interest, colour and low maintenance. Your planting plan should indicate the positions of all trees and shrubs, herbaceous or ground-cover plants, bulbs and annuals, and it should also state how many of each are required. As the plan will be used not just as a basis for ordering the plants but for allocating their planting positions after delivery, it must be accurate and easy to understand. A planting plan on paper also helps to produce a better composed and more balanced effect and will also serve as a record of what has been planted.

Developing a detailed planting plan usually follows the acceptance of the layout plan by the client. There is absolutely no point in wasting your time and the client's money in producing a detailed planting plan until the garden layout has been agreed. In preparing your layout plan, you may have made decisions about the planting that ought to be adhered to – for example, 'scented border' or 'shady border to include ferns and bulbs' – and you may, for instance, have committed yourself to using certain types of plants or to including a particular tree or shrub in a border. Clients will often require you to work with existing plants or structures.

As you draw up the planting plan, remember that it is also the designer's responsibility to reject any plants that are substitutes, substandard or incorrectly labelled. This is difficult to do if you are unfamiliar with the plant and have only recently made its acquaintance through a catalogue or book!

## POINTS TO CONSIDER BEFORE PLANT SELECTION

Before you rush into plant selection, there are many points that you should consider. First, reflect on the hard materials used in the layout plan and the period and architectural style of any buildings. The types of plants used should complement these. The size or proportion of the buildings and the space to be planted will affect both the choice of plants and the groupings – you may need strong outline shapes and large groups of a single type of plant to link a large mass of buildings with planting. Aspect, microclimate, soil conditions, site constraints, the client's lifestyle and preferences, colour palette, seasonal effects and budget will all affect your choice, and it is useful to refer back to your site analysis and report to remind yourself of any limitations.

### Quality of light

Think of the quality of light and how it will affect your planting. The latitude will affect the intensity of the light, and shadow patterns and outlines shapes are more clearly defined in some areas, while in others only strong foreground shapes may stand out. Gertrude Jekyll, one of Britain's, most brilliant garden designers, already had poor eyesight when she began drawing garden plans, and she relied heavily on outline shape for her excellent plant groupings.

### Compatible varieties and groupings

The plants you choose ought to be in proportion to their surroundings. Delicate leaf shapes and fragile flowers will look out of place if they have to compete for attention with a modern tower block. The distinctive outline shape of the plants and their form, texture and scent will make your planting groupings memorable and are usually more important than comparatively fleeting flowers.

You should also consider the ecological relationship of the plants. Lavender and rhododendrons will not only look unnatural together, but they require different soil conditions. Keep a plant notebook, and when you visit gardens, write down not only the plants that you like, but also note the companion planting. The effect may be made in the way the plants are grouped, not in the individual plant. Referring back to these plant notebooks may provide you with inspiration when time is short and your imagination is at a standstill.

When you name plants, always use the most up-to-date botanical name, because common names vary widely from country to country.

### Form and texture

The shape or form of a plant and its leaf colour and texture, rather than the flowers, should be the main consideration when choosing plants. This will give contrast and long-lasting visual interest to your designs. Round plants should be interspersed with spiky or tiered shapes, such as yucca or *Viburnum plicatum*, which will relieve a regimented, 'bun' like outline. Try to think of the leaf colour and texture as fabric, contrasting a glossy satin finish, such as aucuba, with the more matt, velvety leaves of, say, stachys.

### Light reflection and absorption

Do not overlook the light reflective or light-absorbent qualities of the leaves. Glossy evergreens, such as *Choisya ternata* or *Aucuba japonica*, reflect the light, while yew (*Taxus*) absorbs it. Using light-reflective and light-absorbent material or introducing silver (*Convolvulus cneorum*) or blue-green foliage (*Euphorbia wulfenii*) into a border can maintain interest without anything being in flower.

### Scent

The scent of flowers is one of the great pleasures of a garden. Try not only to choose a fragrant species, but also to think about the time of day that the plant gives off the perfume. Some plants, such as nicotiana, are heavily scented in the evening, to attract moths, while others, such as *Virbunun carlesii*, can be enjoyed throughout the day. It is often assumed that all roses or honeysuckles will have a perfume, and how disappointing it can be to a client to discover that the particular variety chosen by you does not have this particular attribute.

### Colour

This can be a very emotive subject. Almost every client has a particular dislike – mauve or orange, perhaps – but will be less definite about what they do like. The request for 'lots of colour' is often misleading, and you should always consider the interior colour scheme and try to reflect it in the garden. Entire beds or garden rooms can be planted in blends or contrasts, while an indiscriminate mixture of colour is as jarring to the eye in a garden as it would be in a room or on a person.

### Blends of colours

A scheme in which blends of colour, such as creams moving through yellows to apricot or orange, perhaps highlighted by blue, or by a planting of pale pinks to reds to mauves, can be successful provided that they are appropriate to their surroundings. A bed of pink flowers backed by a red brick wall could look horrific, while the same flowers might be a marvellous contrast to a light-absorbent yew hedge. Foliage borders, too, can concentrate on blends of a single hue – yellows lighting up a dark corner or silvers giving a cooling effect.

### Contrasting colours

A blue-tinged, northern light shows off to advantage the soft pinks, blues and silvers that are popular in so many gardens. Clashes of stronger colours, such as orange and purple, are less familiar but can, if used with discretion, be equally effective and less predictable. So much depends on the backdrop. Sometimes colours follow the current fashion, with perhaps pink flowers backed with green foliage picking up the latest fad from the fashion houses. Clear blues, yellows and reds tend to brighten overcast spring days, and in autumn the more fiery, reddish tints of leaves, contrasting with the purplish-blue of Michaelmas daisies, are effective in crisp, cooler weather.

### Single colours

A garden or garden room that concentrates on a single colour, such as white, can be very striking. It is possible to use not only white flowers, but white-veined or marbled leaves such as *Eryngium bourgatii* 'Oxford Blue', the felted grey-leaved *Stachys byzantina* offset by glossy green foliage, such as the hart's tongue fern (*Phylittis scolopendrium*), can be exciting both for designer and client. There are many other single-colour possibilities, but in all cases a selection of matching and contrasting foliage is needed to carry through and soften the effect.

### Other limiting factors

There will be many functional reasons for plant choice, which will vary with every site, and you should refer back to the site analysis and, if available, your report as *aide-memoires*. The functional considerations could be the need to screen or frame views, provide shade, filter wind or noise or direct circulation.

### Reference books and catalogues

Most designers quickly accumulate a library of reference books and catalogues, and you will probably already have some reliable favourites ready to consult. Often much valuable design time is taken up searching for inspiration, and a more disciplined approach can be to develop the planting plan by looking at the composition of two-dimensional forms on the ground plane, by quickly sketching the horizontal relationship between the proposed plants and their surroundings, and then to build on these to provide the complete spatial plan in three dimensions. These quick sketches can help you to visualize your groupings within their setting before you consult books or catalogues, to which you can refer only to confirm plant suitability and, possibly, spelling.

No two books will agree totally on plant behaviour and characteristics, and there is no substitute for a sound personal knowledge of the plants you have selected. Try not to be too ambitious and, at least to begin with, use popular plants whose attributes and performance have made them well known.

If possible, all plants should be obtained from one reliable stockist, often a wholesale nursery. Garden centres tend to be expensive and are usually less willing to give a discount for bulk orders.

For your embryonic or evolving plan try not to use a catalogue, but think only of outline shapes and textures. Only when your plant positions are on the plan and you have established an overall balance for what you are trying to achieve, should you actually put names to the plants. If you use a catalogue from the beginning, you will have filled up your planting plan before you reach the middle of the alphabet.

### Suppliers

Most garden designers have their favourite, and often fairly local nurseries, many of which will be wholesale. Many wholesale nurseries supply a wide range of stock, but experienced designers will probably also have a filing system for specialist catalogues, broken down into sections such as trees, shrubs, roses, grasses, bulbs and annuals, where they know they can obtain well grown and perhaps unusual plants at a reasonable price.

Sometimes a designer will send out a plant list to several nurseries, asking each to quote availability, size and price. Remember that delivery will be an extra expense, which is cheaper if the nursery is local or if you can collect the plants yourself. Retail nurseries may give substantial discount to designers for bulk or regular orders and it's work asking abut this before you place an order. However, obtaining plants from too many sources is not only time-consuming and therefore expensive, but it also means that the plants may be delivered at different times. It is much easier to execute a planting plan on site if you have your entire palette of plants at your disposal, rather than having to leave gaps for late arrivals.

### Key and skeleton plants

Some key and skeleton plants will be needed to link the planting to the buildings or the surrounding landscape. The key plant should have some quality that makes it stand out as a feature from the rest of the planting. This may be the outline form, as with phormium, the foliage shape of a plant such as fatsia, or simply its colour, as with *Robinia pseudoacacia* 'Frisia'. A distinctive tree or large shrub can ct as a pivot round which the rest of the planting revolves. Although you are working on a flat plan, you need to visualize not only the dimensions of the plants but also their outline shapes and textures.

With the key plants in place you can choose the skeleton plants, those that have a good, year-round outline shape, and here texture will offset the more ephemeral planting.

After your key and skeleton plants are in place, the flowering shrubs may be chosen, although often the best plants are those whose flowers are shown off by their foliage, such as a pink rose with glaucous blue leaves, or a white cistus with glossy green leaves. Try to vary the outline shapes by including plants with spiky, rounded or layered silhouettes.

### Climbers and wall shrubs

These are useful not only for softening structures but also because they can quickly add a third dimension to borders, particularly narrow ones at the base of a house wall. Deciduous border planting can be set off by a backdrop of evergreen *Clematis armandii* or Hedera (ivy) or a blue and yellow colour scheme can be accentuated by the rambling rose 'Goldfinch' and blue *Ceanothus impressus*.

### Herbaceous or ground-cover plants

These plants can be used to soften the overall effect as well as reducing maintenance. Large-leaved plants, such as bergenias or hostas, can contrast with the more delicate foliage of thalictrum, while the woolly, grey foliage of *Stachys byzantina* or a spreading carpet of *Ajuga reptans* may be effective creeping through other plants at the front of a border.

### Bamboos, ferns and grasses

Although they can be invasive, bamboos can give an oriental flavour and the taller varieties can be effective for screening. The inclusion of grasses or ferns tends to give a more natural look. Strictly speaking, they should be classed separately on a plant list, but are often included with other categories.

### Infill plants

Particularly helpful for bulking up a newly planted garden, infill plants can be used temporarily among the permanent planting until it has matured.

Annuals such as *Nicotiana sylvestris* or clumps of forget-me-nots, which self-seed if allowed, can help to cover the soil in the early stages, while cuttings can be taken from the more tender species, such as osteospermum, overwintered in the greenhouse and used again the following year.

### Bulbs, corms and rhizomes

These not only maximize the use of the soil by being planted under other plants, but they can enliven the borders early in the year and may extend the flowering season throughout the summer and early autumn. Summer bulbs such as *Tritelia laxa* can help carry through a blue scheme, while the taller, scented *Lilium regale* can give a paler effect amongst larger plantings.

## STARTING THE PLANTING PLAN

Using your garden layout plan as an underlay, lay a sheet of tracing paper over it and trace off the proposed planting areas. These areas can either remain at their original scale, or they can be enlarged to any desired scale – 1 : 50 or 1 : 100 is usually preferred – but if the site is very large you may wish to show the position of trees and major shrubs only, in which case 1 : 200 or 1 : 500 might be used. Make sure that the outline of the planting area, at whatever scale, will fit comfortably onto your sheet of tracing paper.

Having drawn the outline shape to scale, place your tracing paper over the graph paper backing sheet on your drawing board. Establishing the scale size of a major grid square will help you to relate to the spread of

*How to draw up a planting plan. Use your garden layout plan as a base and trace off the proposed planting areas.*

proposed plants and how much space they will occupy on the ground. At this stage, the exact location of your plan on your tracing paper is not important, because your final drawing for the client will be on a further trace overlay, giving much more information. Label each plant and indicate how many of each species will be planted.

### Height and spread
Not all tall plants need to be consigned to the back of the border. Height should be treated like rhythm and should flow backwards and forwards through the borders with carefully sited 'spot' plants, such as verbascums or foxglove, being allowed to interrupt low

planting and relieving monotony. Most catalogues and reference books give the expected height and spread of a plant after five years, and although this varies enormously (both in the books and in reality), plants should be given sufficient space to allow their natural form to be appreciated, as opposed to being overcrowded, when they mature. Shorter lived plants, such as rosemary, could be used as semi-permanent stop-gaps.

### Key planting
Begin by deciding on the location of your key plants – the feature trees and shrubs that you will use to link the planting with the architecture, hard surroundings or landscape – a tree used to soften the angular shape of, for instance, a pond. Either make large freehand circles with a soft, dark pencil or use compasses or a circle template, although it is quicker to work freehand. Try to balance a proposed tree by drawing a group of three shrubs in the opposite corner. At this stage you should not think about what the plants will be, only about balance and counterbalance.

Groups of a single type of plant should overlap each other.

### Skeleton or structure planting
The next stage is to add the skeleton planting, which will consist of shrubs and climber s to give the garden structure, particularly evergreens, for the winter months. Balance is, again, important. Try to arrange the groups to create movement diagonally from one side of the garden to the other and to help to unify the design. Vary the size of the circles to represent a range of different plant species of

*Add the key plants first – here the tree and the group of three shrubs are placed diagonally opposite. Then work in the structure planting.*

A central dot indicates a shrub

Climber or wall-trained shrub

Draw a line between the centres of shrubs to show adjacent plants of the same species varying size and to show the space that they will occupy on the soil.

### Evergreen and deciduous climbers and decorative shrubs

You will now soften the planting by adding those plants that will play a more decorative role. Try to achieve a ratio of approximately 1 : 3 evergreen to 2 : 3 deciduous plants. Hatch in the evergreens so that you can see the balance.

Choose an evergreen climber for behind a deciduous shrub and vice versa. The tree, shrub and climbing plants will provide the winter scene.

### Decorative planting

The herbaceous or ground-cover plants are added as 'drifts'. Try to draw these as flowing natural shapes, avoiding sharp points. At this stage you are still concentrating only on a balance of shapes. Several of the herbaceous

plants may be repeated as different groups, but what the plants actually are is not decided until the pattern and shapes are complete.

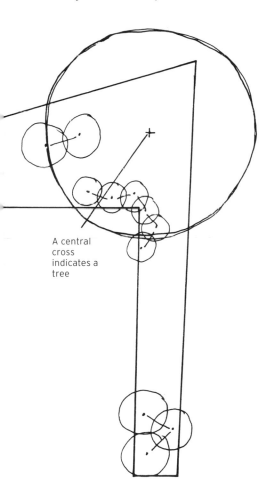

A central cross indicates a tree

*Next, add in the decorative shrubs that will be shown off by the key and structural planting.*

Shade or hatch evergreens

### Herbaceous or ground-cover planting

Once all the skeleton and decorative planting is in place, you can concentrate on herbaceous plants, or those smaller scale plants that will filter through the larger specimens. On your plan show these herbaceous plants as drifts linking the key, structure and decorative planting. Some herbaceous plants may have strong architectural shapes – acanthus and kniphofia, for instance – or bold leaves, such as hostas. Contrast these strong shapes with softer, fluffier plantings and think about how this herbaceous planting will look against the form, texture and colour of your shrubs and climbers. Try to design the herbaceous areas as drifts rather than as blocks, in which different herbaceous plants weave through the beds and appear to merge into one another.

Label as you go along, stating how many of each, balancing deciduous with evergreen and, again, repeating groups diagonally. One of the most common faults in planting plans is lack of repetition or the use of too many varieties. This makes a border look restless and unnatural. Indicate the exact planting position and how many of each with a single line to the centre of the group.

### Bulbs and infill plants

Bulbs or annuals can be indicated by showing their position and numbers with a broken line, or simply by a line pointer indicating where a group would go. Because bulbs and annuals or infill plants are often used under, or to intermingle with, more permanent plants, it is usually easier indicate these with a line or arrow rather than labelling them.

PHLOMIS ITALICA / 2
CLEMATIS 'PERLE D'AZUR' / 1
CARYOPTERIS × CLANDONENSIS / 4
IRIS PALLIDA DALMATICA / 7
GLEDITSIA 'RUBY LACE' / 1
GERANIUM 'JOHNSON'S BLUE' / 5
ANEMONE HUPEHENSIS 'SEPTEMBER CHARM' / 9 + ALLIUM KARAVATIENSE / 12
CAMPANULA LACTIFLORA 'POUFFE' / 9
SENECIO 'SUNSHINE' / 4
STACHYS LANATA / 8
PALLIDA DALMATICA / 6
ROSA 'NEW DAWN' / 1
ANEMONE HUPEHENSIS 'SEPTEMBER CHARM' / 5 + ALLIUM KARAVATIENSE / 8

CEANOTHUS DENTATUS / 1
NARCISSUS 'THALIA' / 50
DEUTZIA × ROSEA / 3
HEBE 'E.A. BOWLES' / 5
IRIS PALLIDA DALMATICA / 5
STACHYS LANATA / 7
SOLANUM JASMINOIDES 'ALBUM' / 1
PAEONIA 'CHINA ROSE' / 7
MUSCARI BOTRYOIDES / 23
CARYOPTERIS × CLANDONENSIS / 3

ACANTHUS SPINOSUS / 5
HEBE 'E.A. BOWLES' / 6
MUSCARI BOTRYOIDES / 25
VITIS VINIFERA 'PURPUREA' / 1
GERANIUM 'JOHNSON'S BLUE'
STACHYS LANATA / 9
HYSSOPUS OFFICINALIS / 4
PAEONIA 'CHINA ROSE' / 4
WISTERIA SINENSIS / 1
SENECIO 'SUNSHINE' / 3

*Finally, draw in herbaceous drifts and areas of bulbs and annuals, label each group of plants. Use Latin names and write in the number of plants in each group.*

N

## PLANT SCHEDULES OR LISTS

Having decided on the plants, take an ordinary jotter or a pad of lined paper and head each sheet according to the listing of the catalogue or the nursery that will be supplying your plants. You may, for example, have one sheet for trees, another for climbers, another for shrubs through to bulbs or annuals. Bamboos, ferns and grasses should be listed separately. You should organize your lists to comply with the format of the catalogue. Put the Latin name of the plant at one side and then the number of plants used in each grouping:

*Bergenia purpurascens:*   4+15+9   Total 28
*Vrburnum tinus:*          3+5      Total 8

Arrange the lists in alphabetical order, and remember to add the words 'no substitutes', to protect yourself against the supplier running out of stock of a certain plant and sending you something inferior or unsuitable instead.

## LABELLING

You are now ready to retrace or redraw your planting plan on a final sheet of tracing paper. With this comes the laborious task of labelling each planting group. Never use the technique of numbering plant groups and giving a separate key that is often found in books – by the time you get to 4, you will have forgotten what 1 was.

### Annotating your planting plan

Always write plant names from left to right. You do not want your client to have to turn the plan upside down to read them.

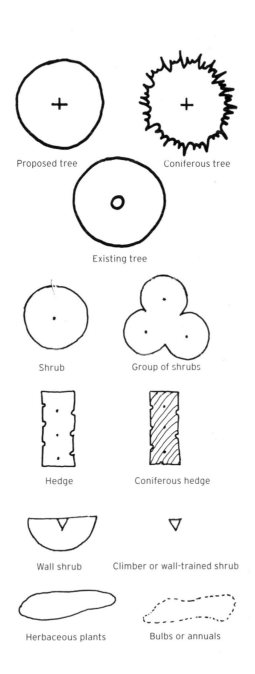

Proposed tree

Coniferous tree

Existing tree

Shrub

Group of shrubs

Hedge

Coniferous hedge

Wall shrub

Climber or wall-trained shrub

Herbaceous plants

Bulbs or annuals

*Common symbols used to represent plants on a plan.*

## KEY TO PLANT SYMBOLS

You may help your client to understand the plan if, alongside it, you provide a key to any symbols that you may have used on the plan. It is best to keep these symbols as simple as possible, both to shorten the time that it takes to draw them and to ensure that the plan looks as uncluttered as possible, which will make it easier to read. Freehand drawing and lettering often give a plan more personality than one created with the aid of expensive transfers.

Plant symbols can be used to help distinguish plants of different character. If you decide to use them, aim for simple, stylised outlines and remember that the primary aims of a planting plan are to indicate precisely what plants are to be used and to show exactly where they should be positioned in the area to be planted. Planting plans are supposed to be working drawings, not ones that show every leaf and flower.

In the symbols illustrated, you can see that the centre points of all trees and shrubs are clearly marked. It is important to show this because it indicates to the existing stem or proposed planting position. The outline shape of each symbol represents the spread of the plant. In the case of a tree, this is the width of its canopy. It is useful to indicate tree canopies, particularly of existing trees, as their spread will affect what you can plant beneath the. If you are intending to plant under trees, you should also show the plants through the tree canopy. Bold lines used for drawing trees can

Conceptual outline shapes

More realistic shapes with line quality incorporated

enhance your plan by helping to give an impression of three dimensions. Normally trees are the most dominant plants in a garden, and they should be drawn with a thick felt tip to indicate this.

## ELEVATION DRAWINGS

It is impossible to convey the vertical detail of planting and how it relates to the surrounding architecture or other visual elements on a flat or horizontal plan. Elevations are the easiest way of demonstrating this. They are quick and straightforward to draw up and can be used to indicate to the client the varying plant shapes and forms. (See also Chapter 9.)

Always indicate on the plan the point from which the elevation has been taken so that your clients can identify what they are looking at and from where.

Choose the location of your cut lines carefully, bearing in mind what you are trying to show. In the example shown here, the planted area chosen for the elevation forms the main view of the garden from the house. When you are drawing up an elevation it can be helpful to work in stages. In the initial stage, the layout and basic forms of trees and shrubs are established. Next the elevation is

*When working up a planting plan think carefully about the shape and form of plants and try to vary these. You can show how your design achieves this by drawing an elevation of a particular area. Whether you are using simple outline shapes or adding more line quality, try to capture the character of the plants you are using.*

enhanced by adding herbaceous plants and climbers and developing the shapes.

The elevation need not be to the same scale as the plan drawing, but if it is different, do not forget to indicate this. Elevations usually look best when they are placed above the plan drawing because the plan is normally larger, and therefore the more dominant of the two. The heavier drawing will look better at the bottom of the sheet.

The elevation can also be used to indicate the long-term changes that will take place in the new garden by overlaying a sheet of tracing paper over the previous drawing to show the anticipated effect of your planting after approximately five years. It may be necessary at that stage to show that some of the original plants may have to be removed. Many of the others will have matured and the space may be overcrowded.

*Top: A part of the plan showing from where the elevation is taken.*

*Middle: The resulting elevation, using simple outlines to represent the approximate height and spread of plants.*

*Bottom: The final elevation, showing plant groups depicted more realistically.*

## PLANTING PLANS: THE FINAL PRESENTATION

This should be the culmination of all your work on the planting plan. First, decide on the size of tracing paper that you are going to use. This will normally be A2 (23½ x 16½in) but will vary according to the scale you have used and the dimensions of the planted area. Next, lay your completed rough or previous workings on the graph paper backing sheet and position it carefully, leaving enough space for the elevation drawing to be shown directly above or below, so that it can be related to your plan.

Remember to leave enough space on the right-hand side for your title block, for the north point and for any notes. You may wish to use the space for notes to describe the thinking behind your planting plans for the same garden, give each area a different title, such as 'Bed A', 'Bed B' and so on, and label your plant list accordingly. Then, when a large number of plants is delivered on site, the plants can be quickly sorted through and allocated to particular beds.

Vary nib sizes according to the size and importance of the plant as described for the layout drawings (Chapter 8). After tracing and drawing your completed plan, it can be effective to use cast shadows, tone or colour on your drawing. Remember to apply colour only after you have had the work photocopied or printed on to a plain paper sheet. Colour may not reproduce from a trace and should always be added to the final printed drawing. If the planted area has been designed to have a particular colour scheme or to look colourful at a certain time of year, this can be indicated by the use of similar colours to enliven the elevation and to help to demonstrate your intention to the client.

However, remember that the plants do not all flower at the same time, and to indicate that they might do would be misleading. The type of finishing treatment you choose will depend on what you have arranged with the client, but it is usually wise to do a little more than he or she actually expects. With experience, you will soon become confident in your ability to communicate your ideas effectively and speedily.

## OTHER WAYS OF ENLIVENING A PLANTING PLAN

### Distinguishing between evergreen and deciduous plants

Show all evergreens with a pencil tone overlaid on the reverse side of the drawing. You should apply the pencil to the reverse side of the sheet so that when it is turned over, a hand moving across the drawing will not smudge the lead. Always move the lead in the same direction and try not to sharpen or change the lead until the shading work is finished.

### Shadows

Shadows can be used to bring depth to a plan by showing relative heights. Check first to see where north lies – the shadows should be in the opposite direction from the sun. The taller the object, the longer the shadow. Shadow effects are discussed in more detail on page 66.

*Below: Techniques for drawing plant shadows.*

*Right: The completed planting plan.*

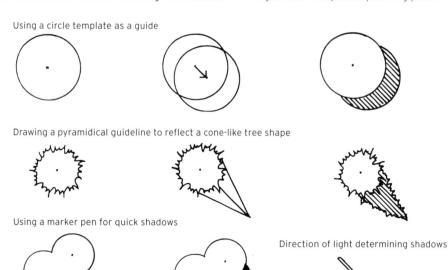

Using a circle template as a guide

Drawing a pyramidical guideline to reflect a cone-like tree shape

Using a marker pen for quick shadows

Direction of light determining shadows

ELEVATION OF SOUTH-FACING BORDER

**NOTES**

**Trees**
Gleditsia 'Ruby Lace'/ 1                    1

**Shrubs**
Caryopteris x clandonensis/ 3,4            7
Deutzia x rosea/ 3                          3
Hebe 'E.A Bowles'/ 6,5                     11
Hyssopus officinalis/ 4                     4
Phlomis italica/ 2                          2
Senecio 'Sunshine'/ 4,3                     7

**Climbers and wall shrubs**
Ceanothus dentatus/ 1                       1
Clematis 'Perle D'Azur'/ 1                  1
Rosa 'New Dawn'/ 1                          1
Solanum jasminoides 'Album'/ 1             1
Vitis vinifera 'Purpurea'/ 1               1
Wisteria sinensis/ 1                        1

**Herbaceous perennials**
Acanthus spinosus/ 5                        5
Anemone 'September Charm'/ 5,9            14
Campanula lactiflora 'Pouffe'/ 9           9
Geranium 'Johnson's Blue'/ 5,5            10
Iris pallida dalmatica/ 5,6,7             18
Paenoia 'China Rose'/ 7,4                 11
Stachys lanata/ 7,8,9                     24

**Bulbs**
Allium karavatiense/ 8,12                 20
Muscari botryoides/ 23,25                 48
Narcissus 'Thalia'/ 50                    50

N.B. All dimensions must be checked
on site and not scaled from this
drawing

**CLIENT**
**MR & MRS WILSON**
**BERKSHIRE**

**DRAWING TITLE**
**PLANTING PLAN**

**DRAWING NO.**
**087**

**DRAWN BY**
**KB**

**REVISION NO.**

**DATE**

**KARENA BATSTONE**
98 Clapham Common Northside
London SW4 9SG
Tel: 071 223 3203

© Karena Batstone 1994

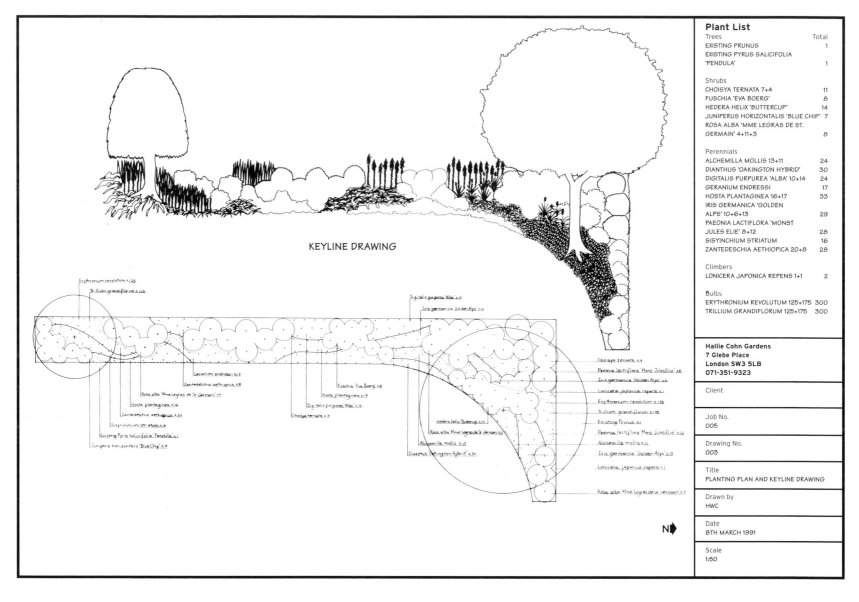

KEYLINE DRAWING

**Plant List**

| Trees | Total |
|---|---|
| EXISTING PRUNUS | 1 |
| EXISTING PYRUS SALICIFOLIA 'PENDULA' | 1 |

| Shrubs | |
|---|---|
| CHOISYA TERNATA 7+4 | 11 |
| FUSCHIA 'EVA BOERG' | 8 |
| HEDERA HELIX 'BUTTERCUP' | 14 |
| JUNIPERUS HORIZONTALIS 'BLUE CHIP' | 7 |
| ROSA ALBA 'MME LEGRAS DE ST. GERMAIN' 4+11+3 | 8 |

| Perennials | |
|---|---|
| ALCHEMILLA MOLLIS 13+11 | 24 |
| DIANTHUS 'OAKINGTON HYBRID' | 30 |
| DIGITALIS PURPUREA 'ALBA' 10+14 | 24 |
| GERANIUM ENDRESSI | 17 |
| HOSTA PLANTAGINEA 16+17 | 33 |
| IRIS GERMANICA 'GOLDEN ALPS' 10+6+13 | 29 |
| PAEONIA LACTIFLORA 'MONST JULES ELIE' 8+12 | 28 |
| SISYINCHIUM STRIATUM | 16 |
| ZANTEDESCHIA AETHIOPICA 20+8 | 28 |

| Climbers | |
|---|---|
| LONICERA JAPONICA REPENS 1+1 | 2 |

| Bulbs | |
|---|---|
| ERYTHRONIUM REVOLUTUM 125+175 | 300 |
| TRILLIUM GRANDIFLORUM 125+175 | 300 |

**Hallie Cohn Gardens**
**7 Glebe Place**
**London SW3 5LB**
**071-351-9323**

Client

Job No.
005

Drawing No.
003

Title
PLANTING PLAN AND KEYLINE DRAWING

Drawn by
HWC

Date
8TH MARCH 1991

Scale
1:50

*In this presentation, the keyline drawing (elevation) will help the client to visualize the finished planting. The designer has carefully selected which groups of plants to emphasize, contrasting perennials with simplified shrub outlines. The result is uncluttered and quick to draw.*

VIEW  A

VIEW  B

VIEW 'A'

VIEW 'B'

*"Matisse inspired"*
*with colours of blue and*
*yellow for summer;*
*boulders, pebbles, water*
*and sculpture!*
*All housed within a moat*
*and wall of flowing water.*

**HM DESIGN**
Helen Miller
**25 BASING WAY**
**THAMES DITTON**
**SURREY KT7 09X**

Job no
*009*

Rev
1

Scale
NOT TO SCALE

Date
23 JANUARY 1993

Drawn by
HELEN MILLER

*These elevations show two views of a 'Matisse'*
*garden, comprised of stone, water, sculpture and*
*herbaceous borders. The designer has achieved a*
*balance of realistic and abstract forms, depicting*
*many of the plants in a stylised way to increase*
*the impact of the design. The simple treatment of*
*the boulders enhances the drawing.*

# CHAPTER ELEVEN

# Enhancing with visuals

Despite all your work in producing a garden layout and planting plan, from which the garden will be built and planted, your client may have difficulty in understanding your concept. Visuals will help you to explain your intent and, in the case of planting plans, can show the anticipated growth rate at different stages.

## PRESENTATION STYLES

For the garden designer, the main purpose of any plan is to communicate ideas to a client. How this is done can vary considerably and the designer usually develops an individual style which can be adapted to the type of work undertaken. The following colour pages show a wide range of work. You should experiment with graphics until you find a method that suits your own ability and which will appeal to your client.

*Right: The two plans show the development of a garden design using a grid system to relate the proposed scheme to the existing house structure. The grid chosen for this site derives from the dominant lines – the corners, the edges of the bay window and the conservatory. These lines are subdivided to create a 1-m (1-yd) grid. The design is then developed using the grid lines as a guide, resulting in well-balanced proportions.*
*A rectangular theme, based on the grid, has evolved for the site. This is appropriate to the style of the house and allows generous proportions for lawn, paved areas and paths. Bringing in the third dimension, a pergola at the far end of the garden provides shade and vertical interest, which is accentuated by the retention of several existing trees.*

Herb garden

Lawn

Terrace for sitting out

Conservatory

Residence

Existing tree

Path

Sitting area for afternoon sun

Steps and paving

Roses, Herbaceous plants, silver foliage plants

Midsummer and autumn border backed by evergreys and evergreens

Low shrubbery cascading over wall

Late spring shrubbery

Evergreen groundcover

Cherry

Magnolia

Proposed siting of statuary on plinth

Climbers on railings

Lime

Conservatory

Lawn

Pear

Yorkstone terrace

Residence

Pergola

Yorkstone paving

Evergreen planting

Wood bench

Shrubbery foliage plants

Lime

New Cherry tree to balance one on far side

Shrubbery evergreens

Trees

Shrubs

Climbers

Perennials

Water plants

Bulbs

Client

Drawing title
PLANTING PLANT

Drawing no.
16.6

Drawn by
K.B.

Date
1.11.95

scale
1:25

KARENA BATSTONE
Garden designer
98 CLAPHAM COMMON NORTHSIDE
LONDON SW4 9SG
071 223 3203

© Karena Batstone BSc 1993

*Right: The layout plan for this small garden shows changes of level and other hard landscaping features. Some indication of the intended planting is given and the two sections show how the garden may look when mature. The drawing has been rendered using coloured pencils applied with varying density to create a feeling of depth. This is further enhanced with the use of projected shadows. When using colour pencils it is easier to anticipate the final effect and avoid clashes of colour if you begin with low tones and build them up gradually.*

Tension wire to support scented climbing plants and roses

Detailed trelliswork to offer court interest and privacy from adjacent garden

Iris bed

Evergreen planting

Shrub rose

Flowering shrubs

PAVED COURT

HOUSE

Perennials

SEATING AREAS

Agapanthus

KITCHEN WINDOW

STORAGE – Shed to be covered in fine gauge chicken mesh as additional support for climbing plants

Winter flowering

Summer planting

Lilies/hostas

GATE

LEVEL 3

LEVEL 2

LEVEL 1

C    TRELLIS    SHRUB ROSE/PERENNIALS    D

A    TRELLIS    PERENNIAL    EVERGREEN SHRUBS    B

*Above: The client may find a garden layout plan difficult to understand. These enticing illustrations for the formal garden clarify the proposals and each sketch is numbered to show the precise location. If you find freehand sketching difficult, these little diagrams can easily be adapted from a book or catalogue, and they may help sell the concept.*

*This axonometric drawing illustrates the circular theme used to give a sense of movement in a rectangular garden. This type of drawing shows how retaining walls and steps create changes of level. It can also be used to check on proposed heights and widths. Loose outline shapes indicate the contrasting form and texture of the planting, while pencil shading has been applied to give a three-dimensional effect. The inclusion of a garden seat gives a sense of scale.*

This page has a planting plan and two photographs, taken a year after planting, that illustrate how a design concept for a garden is realized. Photograph (a) is an overall view of the garden and (b) is the south-west corner.

Top: The planting in this garden has been designed so that the flowering herbaceous plants are set off against a framework of shrubs, incorporating existing ones such as the box square in the foreground. Although the colour scheme is predominantly red, an infill of blue gives interest until the planting matures.

Above: The surrounding ragstone walls and overhanging foliage plants provide a background for this border. At their flowering peak in early summer bulbs are used to vary the colour scheme.

3 ROSA MOYESII
4 COTINUS 'ROYAL PURPLE'
1 PHOTINIA 'RED ROBIN'
30 CROCOSMIA 'LUCIFER'
3 ROSA 'SCARLET FIRE'
11 CANNA – RED/ PURPLE FOLIAGE, 8+3
1 VITIS VINIFERA 'PURPUREA'
8 FOENICULUM VULGARE PURPUREUM
4 PHYGELIUS CAPENSIS
7 GEUM 'MRS BRADSHAW'
7 LUPIN 'RED ROVER'
1 ROSA 'PAUL'S SCARLET CLIMBER'
2 PHYGELIUS CAPENSIS
3 GEUM 'MRS BRADSHAW'
1 VITIS VINIFERA 'PURPUREA'
1 PHORMIUM TENAX PURPUREUM
11 PAPAVER 'INDIAN CHIEF, 5+6
1 ROSA 'CRIMSON SHOWER'
10 SIDALCEA 'CROFTWAY RED', 5+5
7 ROSA 'EUROPEANA', 4+3
13 PENSTEMON 'RUBY', 4+9
1 VITIS VINIFERA 'PURPUREA'
7 HELENIUM 'MOERHEIM BEAUTY', 3+4
3 ROSA 'FRENSHAM', 2+1
1 ROSA 'CRIMSON SHOWER'
11 PAEONIA 'PRESIDENT POINCARE', 3+8
7 ACHILLEA 'THE BEACON'
4 KNIPHOFIA 'CAULESCENS'
12 HEUCHERA 'FIREBIRD'

14 BERBERIS THUNBERGII 'ATROPURPUREA NANA'
7 PAEONIA 'RED FLAG'
25 LILIUM 'BITTERSWEET'
6 COSMOS ATROSANGUINEUS
2 ROSA 'FRENSHAM'
8 LYCHNIS × ARKWRIGHTII
8 ACHILLEA 'THE BEACON'
7 SALVIA OFFICINALIS 'PURPURASCENS'
3 FOENICULUM VULGARE PURPUREUM
8 LYCHNIS × ARKWRIGHTII
8 IRIS 'RED FLASH'
17 BERBERIS THUNBERGII 'ATROPURPUREA NANA'

25 LILIUM PARDALINUM GIGANTEUM
4 ROSA 'AUTUMN FIRE'
1 ACER PALMATUM ATROPURPUREUM
12 LYCHNIS CHALCEDONICA
2 COTINUS 'ROYAL PURPLE'
12 KNIPHOFIA 'FIERY FRED'
7 HELENIUM 'MOERHEIM BEAUTY'
7 OPHIOPOGON 'NIGRESCENS'
1 ACER PALMATUM ATROPURPUREUM
7 MONARDA 'CAMBRIDGE SCARLET'
8 DAHLIA 'BISHOP OF LLANDAFF'
1 PARTHENOCISSUS HENRYANA
9 LYTHRUM 'RED GEM'
2 PHOTINIA 'RED ROBIN'
12 CROCOSMIA 'LUCIFER'
12 EUPHORBIA 'GREAT DIXTER'
7 PAEONIA 'KELWAY'S BRILLIANT'
8 LOBELIA 'QUEEN VICTORIA'
8 EUPATORIUM PURPUREUM
1 DESCHAMPSIA 'BRONZE VEIL'
1 PARTHENOCISSUS HENRYANA
3 ROSA 'EUROPEANA'
8 ASTILBE 'FANAL'
10 DAHLIA 'BISHOP OF LLANDAFF'
3 BERBERIS × OTTAWENSIS PURPUREA
7 PHLOX 'STARFIRE'
10 PHLOX 'PRINCE OF ORANGE'
4 KNIPHOFIA 'CAULESCENS'
11 SCABIOSA 'RUMELLICA'

STONEACRE, OTHAM: PROJECT FOR A RED GARDEN
Designer: Anthony du Gard Pasley

0    1    2    3    4    5

## ORTHOGRAPHIC PROJECTIONS

This is a method in which you draw objects by producing a series of parallel projection lines, giving flat views of everything in the garden drawn to scale. This is done by projecting them up from your plan. An elevation is one type of orthographic projection. Other kinds are axonometric and isometric projections.

## AXONOMETRIC PROJECTIONS

An axonometric drawing is a three-dimensional, measured drawing that, by being projected up from a scale plan, will give height and depth to your design. It will provide a view of the garden as seen from above and at an angle – similar, as it were, to viewing it from a neighbour's second-floor window. It will help you to see how the components of the garden – buildings, walls, steps and fences – relate to each other. If you have forgotten to think through, for instance, the height of a retaining wall or the height of risers and widths of the treads of a flight of steps this will become obvious when you are trying to project them. Once you understand the underlying principle, an axonometric drawing is a quick and easy method of checking your design or any details such as the construction of a pergola or pool. The most difficult task in this type of drawing is to depict plants in a lifelike manner.

The drawing is created by tilting your plan 45º from the horizontal, projecting up all the vertical elements at the same scale as the horizontal elements on the plan and then connecting the tops of the verticals. Note that all the horizontals will be drawn as diagonals, but all the verticals will remain vertical.

**1.** Using your parallel rule and a 45º set-square, fix down your garden layout plan at an angle of 45º with, if possible, the lowest level of the garden or the terrace nearest the bottom of the page.

**2.** Stick a sheet of tracing paper over this.

**3.** Use your scale to measure the vertical lines around the boundaries or the exterior of the site and project up from each corner the height of any structure – building, walls, fence and so on – at these points.

**4.** Use your set-square to join up these points, showing the structure that is nearest to you in a broken line. This will indicate its presence,

*Begin your axonometric drawing by projecting up boundary walls (stages 3 and 4).*

POOL

LAWN

GRAVEL

HOUSE

but allow you to 'see' through it on the drawing. Your garden plan will now have become three-dimensional.

**5.** Proceed in the same way with the interior of your plan starting at the lowest level or terrace, which should, if possible, be nearest to you then work up gradually through each construction and change of level. Some more distant features may be hidden behind those in the foreground. At present show only hard landscaping; the plants can be added later. In this drawing each vertical measurement should be taken from the level of your starting point, but if your garden includes several changes of level, it may be easier and quicker, once the first level has been drawn, to slip the tracing paper overlay up or down to adjust to the height of the new level. This will save having to remember to add on, or subtract from the earlier dimensions each time.

All circles on your plan, such as rounds pools, pots or tables, will appear as true circles in an axonometric projection, although they will need to be set up to find the centre point of what will become a raised circle.

**6.** When you have finished drawing all the hard landscaping, including pots, pergolas and garden furniture, there may be so many lines that your drawing looks rather confused. It is sometimes easier to lay a further sheet of tracing paper over the drawing and trace only the lines that you actually want.

*Projecting up internal structures (stage 5).*

*Plants added on an overlay (stage 7).*

**7.** The planting can be added to the same sheet or done on an overlay, the two being combined for the final drawing. Begin by moving to the lowest part or terrace of the garden and locate the planting position of an adjacent tree (or shrub). Project a vertical line up from the centre point of the trunk to the height of the top of the tree, marking on the trunk the point at which the centre, draw a circle to indicate the width or spread o f the tree canopy. Normally the tree canopy will narrow at the top of the tree, so you should draw another circle, using the tallest point of the tree height as the centre of the circle. Join up the two. This will leave only a small amount, or none, of the tree trunk showing, and while it may look a little odd, it is correct. Proceed in the same way for the other trees and shrubs.

**8.** Climbers and herbaceous plants are normally indicated by showing an outline of their height and spread. Avoid confusing the drawing with too much detail of stems, leaves and so on.

Axonometric gridded paper of different scales is available from good artists' shops and can be very helpful in setting up an axonometric projection.

*The completed axonometric drawing, combining hard landscape structures and planting.*

*Examples of completed axonometric drawings.*

*Taxus*

Existing
*Quercus suber*

Primitive
topiary

*Rosa gallica*

Gravel path

Arbor
with honey-
suckle and
roses

Turf bench

Entrance to
garden

Flowery mead

Brick steps

*For this visual of a medieval garden, complete with honeysuckle arbours and flowery mead, the designer has provided an appropriately detailed drawing. The sense of realism has been enhanced by showing individual flowers and leaves. The existing oak, positioned at the entrance of the garden, helps to emphasize the feeling of enclosure.*

In this design for a city garden an axonometric
drawing clearly shows the proposed changes in
level. A series  of decking platforms, which appear
to float over a deep pool, descend gradually to a
gravelled dining and sitting area. The whole
garden is surrounded by trellis and heavily planted
to give an atmosphere of privacy and seclusion.

This axonometric drawing shows how the geometric ground plan of this garden has been overlaid by lush, varied planting, chosen to be enjoyed at close range. Notice how the nearside fence has been drawn in to demonstrate how it will be clothed with a profusion of climbers, maximizing interest in the limited space.

## ISOMETRIC PROJECTIONS

This is similar to axonometric but instead of a 45º set-square, you will need to use a set-square with angles of 30º and 60º. If a plan includes shapes at 45º, such as in a diagonally themed design, an isometric plan will show more than an axonometric one. In fact, the projection can be taken at any pair of angles that add up to 90º, even 75º and 15º as long as the angles are adhered to once they have been chosen.

In projections other than axonometric projections, circles will appear as ellipses, and to achieve this you may need to set up a rectangular framework of straight lines or use an ellipse template.

*Changes of level can add enormous interest to a garden by defining different areas. In this suburban garden the lower paved area has been provided with a focal point – the fountain head – while in the upper part of the garden abundant planting provides the interest. With an isometric projection one appears to be viewing the site from a lower position than in an axonometric projection. This may make isometrics more appropriate for gardens of low buildings.*

*In this asymmetric design for a long, thin garden the site has been divided into an area for dining and another for sitting out. The sandpit, slightly sunken below the decking, has been designed for easy conversion to a pool when a sandpit is no longer needed.*

## PERSPECTIVE DRAWINGS

A perspective drawing is also three-dimensional but unlike a projection it gives a realistic view of the garden as seen from a chosen point and reproduces what is seen in real life. Any part or parts of the garden can be chosen for a perspective drawing, and two sketches usually accompany an average plan. It does not matter if your first attempts at perspective are fairly rough. With practice they should soon communicate your design concept.

A one-point perspective is the simplest to draw. It means that the garden, or part of it, is viewed head-on from a fixed point, called the standpoint. From this fixed point, all parallel lines converge into an imaginary point on the horizon, called the vanishing point, which is located on a plane known as the picture plane.

### Preparing a perspective drawing

**1.** Fix a sheet of tracing paper over your plan. Using your garden layout plan, choose the area that you wish to depict by choosing your standpoint and your picture plane.

**2.** Draw a central line, the sightline, from the standpoint to your picture plane, which will be in the centre of your cone of vision, or the splay of view that is being depicted in the drawing. This must be nor more than 60º wide.

**3.** Draw an elevation of the view and establish an eyeline on the picture plane. This will be a horizontal line at a level at which your eye might rest naturally. This may be 1 metre (1 yard) or more from the ground. If you are viewing the garden from a balcony or upstairs

*After selecting a standpoint and picture plane on the plan (stage 2), draw an elevation of the chosen view and establish an eyeline on the picture plane (stage 3).*

window, it might be 4 metres (4 yards) high. The point at which the eyeline and the sightline intersect is the vanishing point.

**4.** Now draw a line from the vanishing point through each corner of the picture plane.

**5.** Divide up the horizontal and vertical sides of the picture plane at fixed intervals – perhaps every 1 metre (1 yard) – and draw lines from the vanishing point through the fixed points.

**6.** Go back to your plan and measure the distance on the plan between the standpoint and the picture plane.

**7.** Mark this on the eyeline to either side of your vanishing point.

**8.** From that mark, draw a line through to the nearest lower corner at the picture plane, and continue drawing it across your 1 metre (1 yard) radiating lines.

**9.** At the point where your diagonal crosses each radiating line in the ground plane of the projection area, draw in a horizontal line to establish one more grid on the ground plane.

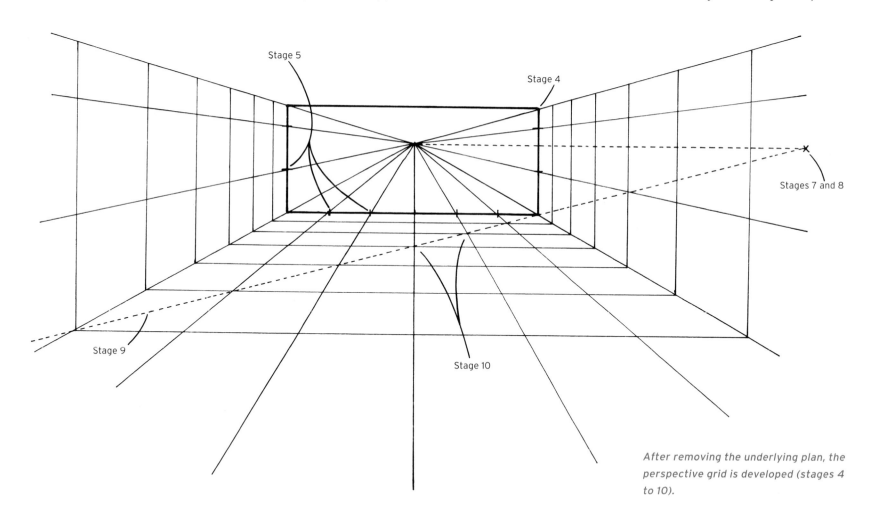

Stage 5

Stage 4

Stages 7 and 8

Stage 9

Stage 10

*After removing the underlying plan, the perspective grid is developed (stages 4 to 10).*

**10.** Construct a vertical 1 metre (1 yard) grid by drawing a vertical line perpendicular to each horizontal grid line at the edge of the ground plan.

**11.** Transfer your garden layout plan to this grid.

**12.** You are now ready to project the elevation drawing forwards using your vertical grid to determine the correct heights of each element on the drawing.

**13.** Link up all the sides of the objects by following a line from each elevate point to the vanishing point.

**14.** To work up a final drawing, lay over a further sheet of tracing paper and trace over the drawing, eliminating the grid lines to show all objects, including trees and shrubs.

To help bring your perspective to life you can use shadows and reflections, varying the thickness of your pens or pencils. Treating the plant material in different ways can give the

*Transfer your garden layout plan on to the ground plane grid.*

impression of form and texture, and the inclusion of people will help your client to identify with scale. It is worth mastering perspective so that you can present your client with an enticing drawing.

Two-point perspective is used to draw objects that are at an angle rather than head-on to the viewer. It is a more complex method of construction and is rarely needed by the garden designer.

All these lines lead back to the vanishing point

*On an overlay, extend up the vertical elements using the vertical grid to determine correct heights (stage 12).*

*The finished perspective with plants added.
Note how the realism of the drawing has been
increased by giving more detail and textural
interest to the plants in the foreground than
to those further back.*

This perspective drawing was achieved by
sketching over an enlarged photograph of the
existing site. When there are elements in the site
that will remain unchanged – such as the house
and mature trees – this method is an effective way
of explaining proposals.

This detailed drawing has been drawn up to demonstrate the profusion of plants intended for the site. When creating visuals of this kind it is better to concentrate on the impression given by the drawing as a whole, rather than attempting to represent every plant accurately.

*The inclusion of the house in a visual often helps to give a sense of scale and may be useful in showing how the design will relate to existing features.*

## SKETCHING OVER PHOTOGRAPHS

This is probably the simplest method, but it does not produce quite the same professional finish. However it is a quick and easy way of presenting 'before' and 'after' effects, and it can also be used to illustrate a report. If you intend to use this technique, it would be sensible to take suitable photographs when you make the survey which usually means taking carefully composed shots of the garden as viewed from the house, and a view looking back towards the house from the opposite end of the garden. The site itself and your immediate assessment of it will probably suggest other shots that you might use.

SLR or digital photography can be used, with the images printed and used as they are, or enlarged. The prints can also be enlarged and reproduced on paper with a photocopier, which is cheaper but not so effective.

*Sketches over photographs are useful for communicating ideas to your clients. They are both quick to draw and easy to understand.*

### Preparing the sketch

**1.** Fix your images or photocopy to your backing sheet

**2.** Lay over it a sheet of tracing paper.

**3.** Refer to your plan and trace over all objects shown in the photograph that you wish to retain. By referring back to your survey it should be possible to gain an idea of the scale at which you are drawing. You will achieve the best effects by drawing in ink, varying your nib sizes for both 'before' and 'after' effects.

**4.** Using another sheet, refer to your garden layout plan and draw your proposals. You may be able to draw them almost to scale. If, for instance, you know the height of an existing garden shed, a proposed pergola could be shown at the same height. Continue until you are satisfied that everything you propose is shown.

## MOOD BOARDS AND CONCEPT BOARDS

### What are they used for?

Mood boards are often used by interior designers to show the mood, style or look that they wish to achieve; and garden designers can adapt a similar technique. A very effective form of visual stimulus, mood boards are usually a presentation tool, but can also form the basis for a client/designer discussion about the design and about materials to be used. Usually worked up after the garden layout and planting plan are complete, the boards can be used to establish a mutual understanding between client and designer.

Occasionally concept plans will also be presented as mood boards, such as landscaping proposals in the form of photographic images and computer graphics to indicate to potential clients – perhaps committees, architects or property developers – how the outdoor space will be used.

Usually a large lightweight board covered with images of spatial ideas and planting, the mood board can indicate whether the design is classic or contemporary, the interplay between materials, colours and plant combinations and how the concept will change the seasons.

### How to make a mood board

Until recently, mood boards were made by sticking down a selection of images cut out from magazines or catalogues, together with occasional mounted samples of lightweight paving materials or soft furnishings. Access to the internet and to digital photography scanning have allowed the presentation to become slicker and more sophisticated, but the aim is still the same – to focus on portraying the main elements of the design arranged in a similar layout to your plans.

### Materials required

- Lightweight or foam (featherlite) board (two pieces as you will need extra for mounting).
- Heavy-duty coloured backing card.
- Double-sided sellotape or spray-fix glue.
- Scalpel, ruler and metal cutting edge.
- A photographically reduced or smaller version of your garden layout plan.
- Selection of images, samples, paint cards, swatches of material, brochures and catalogues.

### Guidelines

**1.** Use a sheet of graph, tracing or layout paper to set out all the different elements before you progress to the boards. Move things around until you are happy with the layout.

**2.** Place your reduced plans centrally, and locate the other elements around it in the same sequence as on your plan.
OR
**3.** Arrange your images and samples in the general order of the space – for examples, paving at the bottom, furniture, trellis, water, lawn and planting in the middle, and pots or overhead sun umbrellas above. By grouping similar items together you will have a clearer idea of how they interrelate than by sticking your samples around at random.

**4.** The amount shown of your samples should reflect how material will take up in reality. For example, avoid filling up your board with paving or an image of particular plants if they are barely used.

**5.** Paint cards and swatches of material can be used to indicate the colours of walls or shades of flowering plants.

**6.** Keep a file of useful materials and images so that you don't need to spend time collecting them afresh for each mood board.

**7.** Remember to leave space for your title block and any other information that should link your mood board with your other plans.

**8.** Once you are satisfied with the position and layout of every item, stick down your coloured backing card, if you like, onto lightweight board. The colour of this card should be chosen to appeal to the client and set off the samples.

**9.** Copy your trial layout by moving all items from your graph or tracing paper sheet to the prepared board. Give certain key items importance by mounting them on a further smaller piece of featherlite board and sticking them down.

**10.** Label each item if you wish – often this is unnecessary as you want to create a mood.

**11.** When the layout is complete, stick down your plan, samples and images with double-sided tape or glue.

Remember that once prepared, you may need to transport your work to the client. Devise a secure method of carrying it without damage.

Many clients find it hard to visualise a flat plan. Showing the main elements of hard landscaping and planting on a mood board will convey the concept.

# CHAPTER TWELVE

# Reproducing and presenting work

Most drawings are originated on tracing paper. Alterations may easily be made on it, but it is fragile and there is only one original, so the finished drawing must be copied to give to the client. It will thus become a negative to be photocopied or printed. This reproduction of the original drawing can then be rendered – that is, it may be coloured or treated in such a way as to explain the concept more clearly.

An established designer often has a particular presentation technique, and it is worth spending some time thinking this through, and deciding what overall effect you wish to achieve. There are many ways of presenting work, and the method you choose will be determined by the intended recipient and the available budget.

## HOW TO USE YOUR PENS AND PENCILS

Methods of drawing and the various media were discussed in Chapter 1 but it may be useful to recap as follows.

Lines may be drawn in pencil, ink or a combination of both, provided that any pencil work is carried out in a fairly hard lead, which will give a crisp line when reproduced. Choose a type of lead that will not smear and, if possible, cover the pencil lines with a clean sheet of tracing paper to avoid smudging if your hand has to move across them.

Technical pen ink, which is normally used with drawing pens, gives a crisp, professional effect, but this comes only with continued practice. There are several recommended sequences which help to give a good finish. This is the most commonly used one:

**1.** Work out nib sizes for all drawn items before commencing the drawing – for example, 0.7 for boundaries, 0.5 trees.
**2.** Starting with the horizontal lines, draw them in with the thickest pen nib size to be used on the drawing.
**3.** Draw in all vertical lines with the same fine nib.
**4.** Draw in all other lines.
**5.** Drawn in all the horizontal lines in the next nib size.
**6.** Repeat this exercise with all vertical and other lines.
**7.** Decrease the nib sizes until all work right up until the thinnest nib size has been executed.
**8.** Work over the final drawing as little as possible by covering the paper or sections not currently being worked on with clean tracing paper.

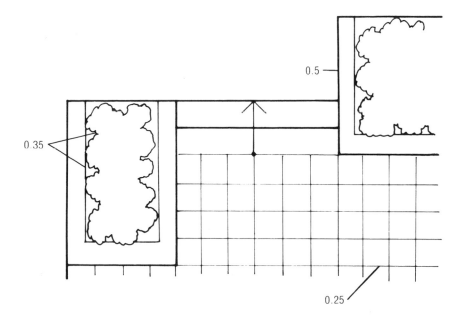

0.5

0.35

0.25

**Common faults when using technical pen ink**

- Very fine ink lines may not reproduce when printed.
- Tense or shaky hands give an uneven effect.
- If the surface of the tracing paper has to be worked over, either by scratching out with a scalpel or by using an eraser, future lines drawn in ink may tend to bleed unless the surface has been restored; the best way of doing this is to burnish the paper with your thumb nail or to move down a nib size.
- If ink is used directly over pencil lead, the lead may prevent the ink from being absorbed evenly by the paper, resulting in an uneven or smudgy line; trace the final drawing over a completed drawing or series of smaller drawings.
- Because inferior quality tracing paper will not stand up to being worked on, use a medium or stout thickness for final drawings.
- Because inferior quality tracing paper will not stand up to being worked on, use a medium or stout thickness for final drawings.
- Do not use coloured pens or pencils on tracing paper because colour may not reproduce when printed or it may cause the tracing paper to stretch or buckle, which will show when reproduced.

*After working out the nib sizes to be used for different elements, start inking in using your finest nib size. Draw all the horizontal lines first, then the verticals and then all other lines. Repeat this exercise with the thicker nibs until you have completed the drawing.*

## REPRODUCING THE DRAWINGS

All final tracing paper drawings, whether of the garden layout plan or of sections or details, will need to be reproduced for the client and the contractors. Sometimes several copies of each are required, to be given to the different contractors or professionals involved. These final drawings will have taken many hours of work and would be costly to redraw. Therefore, each final tracing paper drawing should be classed as an original, and treated with respect.

Store them flat in a plan chest away from excessive heat, damp or sunlight, and take them out of your office in a closed portfolio or rolled in a drawing tube, having made sure that each one has your name, address and telephone number written clearly on the outside so that it can be returned if it is lost or mislaid. Do not send or take them to the reprographic office or printers unprotected and rolled up with only an elastic band or piece of masking tape holding them together. Rain may damage them or the perspiration from your hand may be absorbed by the tracing paper and will then be reproduced on your drawing.

There are three main ways in which your original drawings can be reproduced, but you should understand the differences so that the reproduction will serve its purpose. The methods are copy negatives or prints (dyelines or photocopies).

### Copy negative

This is a reproduction of the drawing as a negative, but this method has now been largely superseded by photocopied prints. It is usually produced on:

- **tracing paper**, when it is hard to tell which version is the original
- **lacquered tracing paper** on which the original is printed on the reverse of the drawing and which is easily torn or damaged
- **sepia film**, in which the drawing is also printed on the reverse side, but which is stronger and less easily damaged.

Copy negatives can be useful if, when the hard landscaping drawing has been completed, you want this to remain as an original but want to draw the planting plan on an exact copy. If the plan is copied, the original can remain as the hard landscaping drawing, perhaps to be copied again before any revisions or alterations are made on the original. If you do, you will no longer have a record of what you have done, and your client may well decide, despite having requested a revision or alteration, that it is best to return to the original design.

Before beginning to scratch out or erase any unwanted material on copies of the originals, check whether the work has been printed on the front or reverse side by testing a small area. If you attempt to scratch anything out without making this test, it is all too easy to end up with a large hole. If the original has been copied on blue intense film, the original may be easily distinguished because it will have been printed on the reverse side in brown, while new work carried out in ink will show up as black. When they are copied, however, the two different colours of ink will reproduce the same.

### Prints

There are two main ways in which copies of the original can be printed on to paper – dyelines and photocopies.

### Dyelines

In modern reprographic offices, the dyeline print has been largely superseded by the photocopy, but in some ways dyeline prints are preferable – they are in cheaper and the finished effect is less harsh. The dyeline process needs a transparent negative – i.e., the drawing on a tracing paper – to be passed through rollers in contact with diazo paper, which is sensitive to ultraviolet light. The roller is a tubular lamp, which emits this ultra-violet light. Good ink originals or negative come up as almost black lines on white paper, while fainter pencil drawings may show some back-ground tint. This can be a grey or bluish tone and the technique used to be called a blueprint. The roller machine may need to be adjusted to give a lighter or darker contrast, and often a good printer will test a strip to begin with, then adjust the machine before printing the complete sheet. However, if your final drawing consists of pieces of paper which have been stuck down with tape, these will show up on the dyeline, although not on photocopies.

### Using colour on dyeline prints

If the drawing is to be used for presentation work or to give to your client, it should be as crisp as possible, and colour or tone may need to be applied afterward. When colour is to be added, the original should be printed on heavier paper, because felt-tip pens or watercolours can make lightweight paper buckle. Reprographic offices do not always hold stocks of this thicker paper, and it must either be ordered in advance or brought in with the original drawing and given to the printer. If watercolours are to be use, it may be best to execute the original pencil so that the ink lines do not overrule the pastel shades. Do not have the original reproduced on watercolour paper as the ink reproduction will not adhere firmly to the thicker paper.

Originals can be printed on a wide range of papers – cartridge, ozalux, which gives a wipeable effect with dull sheen, but on which colour can be difficult to apply, or art grain, which gives an antique or bumpy effect, the ink reproducing in dark brown as opposed to black, which can be appropriate for historic sites. Coloured card can also be used, but this must be thin enough to pass through the rollers.

### Photocopies

This is now the most usual method of reproduction, although few machines will take the largest paper sizes. Photocopying is a photographic process and produces a crisp drawing. Again, the copy can be made on different types of paper, provided these will pass through the

*Folding techniques for standard paper sizes to ensure that the title block remains visible after folding.*

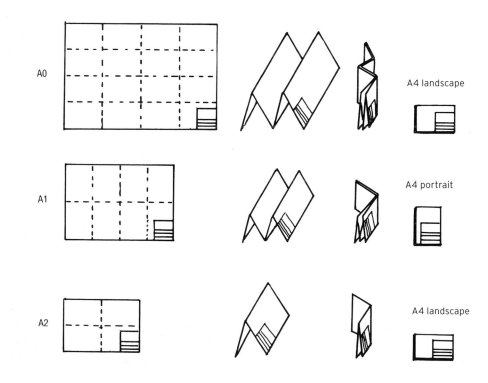

A0

A1

A2

A4 landscape

A4 portrait

A4 landscape

machine, although the ink often does not hold on heavily textured paper.

## Reductions or enlargement

The original drawing may also be reduced or enlarged. You may need to do this because the original drawing is to be reproduced as part of a matching set, perhaps to fit into a portfolio in which the other original drawings have been carried out on a different sized sheet or at a different scale.

A drawing can often look crisper and more professional when it is reduced, although it is important that the content remains clear and the handwriting is legible.

Many photocopying machines have a facility for reducing or enlarging, but before you commit a drawing to be altered in size, make sure that any writing will still be legible. Reductions sometimes improve the overall appearance of a drawing, but if the handwriting is shaky, enlargements will emphasize this. Do a test run to make sure that the process will suite the work and the writing.

Reducing or enlarging will also alter the scale of the drawing, so any notes on scale size will need to be erased or removed before the copy is made, and the adjusted scale – perhaps 1 : 50 reduced to 1 : 100 – written in afresh. A graphic scale will reduce correspondingly.

## Microfilm

Some large practices record drawings on microfilm, which is a photographic process by which miniature transparencies are made of the drawings. This method of storage takes up little space but is expensive and unlikely to be used by many private designers.

## Finishing processes

Once copies of the drawing have been reproduced as dyelines or photocopies, they may be toned, coloured, mounted and sealed, or encapsulated – your choice will depend on how the work is to be presented to the client.

After the copies have been printed, they should be folded or taken or sent as required, but if the plan and the visuals have been printed on thicker than normal paper, you may not wish to fold them. With normal dyeline or photocopied plans or drawings, the paper should be folded so that the lower right-hand corner contains an informative title block. The folding of plans can indicate to a fellow professional the training and experience or lack of it. Knowing how to fold, or unfold a plan is important when you are struggling to open it on a windy, exposed site, or when you are folding a large batch of drawings to send to the various people involved.

It is always better to talk a client through a plan rather than to send it through the post, leaving the client to make his or her own interpretation. Many clients are unwilling to admit that they cannot read a flat plan, and even though it may be accompanied by visuals, there are always points that you should clarify personally.

## COLOURING AND RENDERING YOUR PLANS

### Applying colour

Plans usually look more enticing with some added colour but this needs to be applied sensitively or it will have the opposite effect. Colour should be added to the plans after they are reproduced as photocopies or prints and a heavier duty print paper is recommended so that it will not buckle when coloured. Always ask for several copies in case you make a mistake and remember that if you stack one sheet on top of another the colour may bleed through to the sheet below.

There are three main mediums:
• coloured pencil or felt tips
• watercolour
• pastels

Whatever medium you choose, it is worthwhile spending time in a good art shop choosing a realistic range of colours. Consider what you want to show – better to be selective and only apply colour to a few prominent areas, such as paving, lawn, water or planting. Use earthy shades of browns, greys and greens, or echo the colours of your flowering plants, perhaps in cool or hot colours. Particularly when using a pencil, remember that very few surfaces are one colour – even paving or lawn will have a variation of shades or tones. Paving, for example, may be indicated by using both reddish brown and a grey or yellow crayon to achieve a multi-tone effect. Always experiment on a scrap of paper before starting work on your plans.

### Coloured pencil or felt tips

The strokes of these should always be applied in the same direction. Try leaning your crayons or felt tips against a guiding set square or rolling ruler, moving this guide gradually down your sheet until the area to be coloured is complete. If the colour looks too flat, try adding another shade over the first.

### Watercolour

This can be very subtle and effective, particularly for illustrating planting. Unless you are experienced in using watercolours, you may find it easier to use watercolour pencils – these are applied as coloured pencils, and then washed over with a moist paintbrush. Using too much water will make the paper buckle.

### Pastels

Another attractive and subtle method, but as pastels are easily smudged, work with a protective tissue under your hand and spray with a fixative when finished.

### Rendering

Rendering can be used in combination with applying colour, and is a method of indicating the texture of materials. Rough stone for instance, can be shown by applying the colour over a small sheet of sandpaper or corrugated paper placed behind your plan. If you become adept at rendering, you will begin to collect odd pieces of textured card or old linen book covers to use under your plans.

Pencils and pastels can both be smudged with a cotton wool bud or tissue to merge the colours, and adding pencil shadows can also give a more realistic appearance.

It is wise to allow at least one hour to apply colour to a drawing before presenting it to your client.

## PRESENTING YOUR WORK

The most commonly used methods of presenting your work are:

- **a folded dyeline print or photocopy of your original** (this is the most usual way of presenting work).
- **an extra-stout print,** which is more expensive but may later be framed by the client and should not, therefore be folded.
- **a portfolio,** containing a variety of presentations, including plans, photographs and so on, which is normally used to obtain future work.
- **a print mounted on stiff card or hardboard and heat-sealed around the perimeters** for exhibition or display purposes.
- **a print, possibly reduced or enlarged, encapsulated in clear, firm plastic,** which is a lighter but very durable way of displaying and storing exhibition drawings.

### Dyeline prints

When they are exposed to light dyeline prints fade quickly and can soon become yellow and unreadable. To prevent this they should be stored flat in a clean, dry and dark place. A plan chest is ideal, but a cupboard or drawer will suffice. Work can also be stored in a flat portfolio, which can be slipped under a desk or bed.

### Photocopies

Photocopies do not fade so easily, but they should be stored in a similar way.

### Extra-stout prints

Extra-stout prints that have been rendered or coloured can be very effective, and they may be used to present the client with more sophisticated work. The garden design may sometimes be commissioned as a retirement or anniversary gift, and a drawing printed on this thicker paper gives the recipient the option of having the work framed or mounted as a record of the occasion.

### Portfolios

Compiling a portfolio can be an effective way of displaying completed designs that can be shown to future clients to illustrate the type of work they may expect from a designer. Clients can look through the portfolio, perhaps pointing out a design that appeals to them. As each job is completed, the relevant drawings can be slipped into a portfolio, drawings or prints can be enlarged, or, more usually, reduced. Photographs of the site before work begins and after completion can also be mounted on card, perhaps with descriptive captions, to show future clients what can be achieved. The 'before' and 'after' photographs can also be used as a

*A typical A2 portfolio.*

*In this garden plan the dominant decking is softened by planting. Applied to the photocopy or dyeline print, colour is crucial to defining the different features. Coloured pencils have been subtly blended to give a watercolour effect.*

*Based on circles, this layout plan relates the large terrace to the rest of the space. Sensitive colouring and shading helps enliven the drawing.*

record of the quality of work carried out by the contractors. Costs of the various elements—paving, walls, planting and so on – could also be included so that a future client can judge the level of costs involved. If you do this, include the date of execution, as these costs will not remain static.

## EXHIBITING WORK

If work is to be exhibited, perhaps at an international flower show or art exhibition, it may be necessary to have it mounted and framed, or heat-sealed, which can be particularly important if the exhibition is to be held outdoors, when a damp atmosphere can have a catastrophic effect on paper. Even if the display is under canvas, damp can still ruin drawings. An alternative method is to have the work encapsulated or sealed within two sheets of clear plastic. The drawings remain light to transport and to store, and the sealed work can be mounted on a wall with adhesive stickers. The overall effect of the work will often depend on the background against which it is exhibited, so this should be taken into account when a display is planned. It is best to find out from the exhibition organizers exactly what space is available and what it consists of – whether it is nothing more than a bare stretch of grass on which you will need to erect your own display, or a background of portable lightweight screens. The display can be drawn to scale in diagrammatic form so that the sequence can be followed.

If work is to be submitted for hanging, then this diagrammatic plan should accompany it, including clear instructions and leaving no margin for error by those organizing the

display. A separate board, with the name of the designer or the title of the work, may be mounted above the drawings and occasionally a small box for printed cards for interested viewers can be included. Much future business can be generated by exhibiting at appropriate events, and the display should be as professional and distinctive as possible.

Number each piece of artwork on the reverse side

Rough scaled drawings show where each piece of artwork will be located on the display boards

*Planning the layout for an exhibition.*

Holder for name cards

*The final display.*

# CHAPTER THIRTEEN

# Establishing your own practice

The size and way in which a garden design practice operates can range from a small, part-time consultancy to an international practice that designs and builds gardens. Some designers begin by replanning their own garden, then go on to work for admiring friends and aquaintances until they have built up their own client list. Others have trained through landscape architecture or garden design schools, horticultural colleges or by gaining practical experience in a landscape design practice.

## FINDING YOUR CLIENTS

When you are established, recommendation will probably come by word of mouth, as satisfied clients recommend your service to their friends and colleagues. Initially you will need to sell yourself. How you do this will largely depend on where you operate and the type of housing in your neighbourhood, because it is likely that your first clients will be local. Advertising can be expensive, so it must be well targeted. You must also make sure that what your particular consultancy can offer stands out from other advertisers. It is often more effective to seek editorial coverage or to have a journalist write about gardens you have designed. You may even need to write the article yourself, or you may be commissioned to provide a regular feature in a newspaper or journal. Occasionally garden centres or nurseries need a designer to help their customers plan their gardens, or interior designers, builders or architects may require someone with specialist knowledge. Many clients come through social occasions with friends or acquaintances suggesting that you might like to pop round for a drink and give them a few ideas. It is, however, rarely wise to work for friends, and if you wish to be treated seriously, it is best to give your name and address, or give a card to be followed up later by a phone call.

## FEES

To start up your own practice you must be confident that you have enough ability and practical experience to justify charging fees for your time. Although there are a variety of possible arrangements, most designers charge on a consultancy basis of a set fee per hour or per day, to which must be added travelling time and costs such as petrol, parking, wear and tear on use of car and son on. Other chargeable expenses, such as film and developing photographs of the site, dyeline prints and photocopies, printing of reports or preparation of presentation boards, should also be added. Remember to keep all the receipts.

Your business card or brochure should state who you are and what service you can offer. It should be followed by an initial consultation, for which you may or may not charge, to discuss the project and how you would charge for your services. A letter summarizing the meeting should follow. This should state the scope of your work and what and when you intend to charge for it. A client normally prefers to have some idea of your total charges and of the building and planting costs at the outset. Showing your portfolio of previous work can help clients understand what is involved, and you may even suggest that they contact your past clients to look at your work.

Most designers work to a scale of fees, which indicates the different stages in working up a plan. It may include the following headings:

- **the initial consultation:** a visit to the client's garden for an initial consultation may or may not be charged, or may be deducted from the overall charge if you are engaged.
- **a written report,** which is optional, but is often the basis for a garden layout plan.
- **the garden layout plan** will show proposed areas of hard landscaping, such as paving,

walls and steps, planting areas, together with suggestions for enhancing the scheme with pools or statuary where applicable.

- **a detailed planting plan** will give the botanical names of individual plants required, together with the quantities and costs.
- **the preparation of construction documents**
- **the preparation of specification documents**
- **project supervision**
- **aftercare and maintenance**

You may employ a draughtsman, whose time will be charged at a lower rate, to help with some of your drawings, or you may need to call in specialist advice, such as a tree surgeon or water specialist, who may invoice the client direct. Most clients prefer to know exactly what costs are likely to be incurred before any work begins. Remember to invoice your client regularly and to follow up any non-payments.

After your client has accepted your plan, you will need to obtain quotes from reliable builders, who should be supplied with a specification, against which they will quote, of exactly what is intended. It will be your responsibility to write the specification and to pass on you recommendations on the quotes to your client.

## Overheads

In setting your fees, do not overlook how much it is going to cost to run your practice. You will have overheads such as heating and lighting, and you may have other staff, such as a draughtsman and secretary, bookkeepers or accountants. Your reputation will be enhanced if you establish an organized practice at the outset, which can expand as work develops.

## EXECUTING THE WORK

Once a client has accepted the garden layout and the planting plan, where relevant, the building work can begin. Your client should be encouraged to employ you to oversee the work, because a builder's interpretation of your plan may be different from yours. At this stage, there are three ways in which you can be paid:
- on a percentage basis based on the cost of the work
- on a time basis
- by a lump sum

You will agree with the client which of these methods to adopt. The decision will depend on the proximity of the site and the type of construction involved.

If you are supervising the implementation of the work, you should check progress at the following stages:
- **setting out**
- **excavation to remove topsoil and formation levels**
- **spreading materials already on site**
- **testing topsoil and applying herbicides**
- **ground preparation and the application of fertilizer**
- **grass seeding or turfing**
- **hardcore base for paving**
- **laying concrete and paving**
- **excavation of tree pits**
- **delivery and temporary storage of plants and other materials on site; checking that the correct plants have been delivered**
- **placing plants for planting**
- **watering and finishing off**

The builder will normally expect payment in three stages – one-third before work begins so that he can buy the materials, one-third halfway through and the final third on completion – and your charges can be similarly presented. In most cases you will be responsible for passing the builder's accounts for payment by the client, so it is a simple matter for you to send in your account at the same time. Terms of settlement should be 28 days.

## AFTERCARE AND MAINTENANCE

Aftercare, which is usually charged on a time basis, entails occasional site visits, perhaps twice a year for the first three years, to check how the garden and plants are becoming established and perhaps recommending bulbs, annuals or other additions. You may also be asked to arrange a maintenance contract so that the garden is properly cared for while it matures.

For most garden designers the construction and planting of each garden is the exciting culmination of weeks or months of careful planning. The new garden will take time to develop, but the client can enjoy watching it mature knowing that it has been specifically designed to match that particular property. A satisfied client may recommend our services to others and may even ask you to design the garden for a subsequent home. And for you, as the designer of the garden, there can be the pleasure of visiting a client's garden after several years and seeing how your expertise has helped create something beautiful and unique.

# Index